CANADIAN
HERITAGE
COLLECTION

POPULAR CULTURE

Miriam Bardswich & Gerry Campbell

Series Editor
Don Kendal

Ruˇbicon

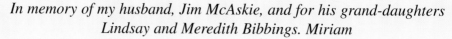

In memory of my husband, Jim McAskie, and for his grand-daughters
Lindsay and Meredith Bibbings. Miriam

To Barbara de Kat, my wife and support. Gerry

*We would like to acknowledge the assistance of Elaine Kelly and Jean Wilkinson of the Lorne Park S. S.
Library and Debbie Keffer of the Hudson's Bay Company. Also, many thanks to Jean-Marc Carisse,
Phil Turner, Nellie Luitkus, Francine Debusschere, Donna & Joan Bardswich, and Cindy Fawcett for
granting us permission to use items from their private collections.*

Rubicon © 2003 Rubicon Education Inc.

Editorial Coordinator: Martine Quibell
Design: Jennifer Drew

National Library of Canada Cataloguing in Publication

(Canadian heritage collection)
Includes bibliographical references and index.
ISBN 0-921156-88-X

1. Popular Culture–Canada–Textbooks. I. Campbell, Gerry
II. Title. III. Series: Canadian heritage collection (Oakville, Ont.)

FC95.4B37 2003   306'.0971   C2003-900352-3
F14021.2.B37 2003

Printed in Canada

COVER

Shania Twain performs during the 36th annual CMA (Country
Music Association) Awards in Nashville, TN, November 2002.
(Photo by Laura Farr/ZUMA Press/KEYSTONE Press. (©) Copyright 2002 by Laura Farr)

Comic Super-hero Captain Canuck was an immediate success
when it debuted in July 1975 (see cover, page 32). Harkening
back to wartime comic heroes such as Johnny Canuck and
Captain Canada, the new hero donned the red and white of
Canada's flag to fight against evil.
(Courtesy Richard Comely)

Five year-old Uzezie Morris smiles for the camera as six year
old Jennine James looks through his headdress at the Cariba
parade in Toronto in August 2000.
(CP Photo/The Toronto Sun/Greg Henkenhaf)

Young hockey fan Reda Ghazal smiles as he watches Canada
celebrate a goal against the U.S. on 24 February 2002 at an
Ottawa electronics store. CBC announced that 8.7 million
people watched the gold medal game that night.
(CP Photo/Jonathan Hayward)

Table of Contents

INTRODUCTION

WE OFTEN THINK of popular culture as entertainment — as movies, television, "top 40" music, and paperback books that appeal to large numbers of ordinary people. These cultural objects, meant to appeal to a mass market, are viewed by some as common versions of "highbrow" or "real" culture. For example, Hollywood films and television are seen as popular forms of live theatre and "art" films; pop music is compared to classical music, and Broadway musicals to opera; and books about celebrities, romance novels, popular magazines, and newspapers are seen as distinct from academic journals and "serious" literature. However, popular culture is much richer and more complex than any such elitist comparison can define. Popular culture includes the expression and depiction of all of the hopes, political ideas, gender roles, ethnic differences, educational experiences, careers, social roles, shared ambitions, clothing, and objects we experience in our everyday lives. They are part of our environment; they are what we are, and they shape how we think and what we become.

In one sense, popular culture is "of the moment." It defines, and is defined by, what is important here and now. It is always new, modern, and current. Even nostalgia, such as a radio station that plays songs from the 1960s, caters to what baby boomers want to hear today. We participate in popular culture when we wear name brand designer clothing, and when we shop in a modern mall or online via the Internet. Popular culture even influences us in the shower! The herbal shampoo we use might be an almost unconscious expression of current environmental concerns.

Popular culture can be explored through common threads such as popular entertainment, books, styles in clothing and design, pastimes, communications media, celebrities, and societal attitudes. One thing we will notice is that a change in one of these areas could signal amazingly rapid changes in the others. For example, a change in popular music might, within months, be mirrored by changes in social attitudes, clothing, and hairstyles, all of which are reflected in media such as ma[gazines], radio and TV shows, movies, gra[phic] design, and commercial artwork. Then, by [the] time this musical influence has affected [all] spheres of society, another trend would li[kely] be evolving within another part of the pop[ular] culture spectrum. Some of these cult[ural] movements turn out to be "flash-in-the-p[an]" fads such as the black bottom dance craze [of] the 1920s, the hula hoop in the 1950s, [the] 1970s pet rocks and lava lamps, and line da[nc]ing in the 1980s. Others, like drive-in mov[ies] last for decades. Some elements of popular c[ul]ture, such as jazz, radio news broadcasts, [and] the automobile, would change with the ti[me] but still remain important.

In the first decade of the 20th cent[ury] most English speaking Canadians were dee[ply] committed to Britain and this was reflecte[d in] the popular culture. By the end of that cent[ury] outside of symbolic ties to the monarchy [and] membership in the British Commonwea[lth,] Canadians were almost wholly under the [cul]tural and economic sway of the United Sta[tes.] Between these two influences, was Can[ada] able, during the century, to develop and ex[pe]rience a unique popular culture of its own?

At the start of the century, Canada wa[s a] young nation of immigrants, most of wh[om] were working the land. For the majority [of] Canadians, life was a routine of hard wo[rk,] religious practice, and family life. What [we] think of as popular culture, linked so firmly [to] media that were just beginning to be invent[ed] was a phenomenon of the future. Howev[er,] change was beginning to occur. With [the] completion of transcontinental railways [and] transatlantic cables came telegraph servi[ce] which made rapid communication possib[le.] The railway also allowed for the growth of [the] mail order business. The Eaton's mail or[der] catalogue made it possible for virtually [all] Canadians to have access to the same go[ods] and fashions that previously had been limi[ted] to city dwellers. No wonder Eaton's became [an] integral part of the Canadian culture during [the] first half of the 20th century.

Bicycles and automobiles made their appearance at the
ı of the 20th century in both urban and rural landscapes.
h new modes of personal transportation came new styles
:lothing such as duster coats, driving gloves, and goggles,
l a range of new activities. It was the start of a whole new
ular culture built around the image of the car and made
.sible by increased mobility.

As manufacturing became increasingly important, there
s a shift of population away from the countryside to the
es. A greater concentration of people with regular work
ırs, even with meagre wages, encouraged the growth of
ap entertainment. The Hollywood-based film industry,
ıch charged people a nickel to watch silent movies, grew in
npetition with inexpensive, live vaudeville shows. Grand
atres, featuring several live shows and films every day,
re built in cities across the country.

Canadian manufacturers such as Heintzman built afford-
e pianos which led to a boom for publishers of sheet music.
is early growth of the pop music industry was fed by catchy
es turned out rapidly in the song factories of New York
y known as "Tin Pan Alley." Soon those tunes were avail-
e on perforated paper rolls for automated player pianos, the
t "records" recorded by some of the biggest stars of popu-
music. At the same time phonograph records were becom-
; popular. Early dictaphone machines were introduced to
ices, but also made recording at home on wax cylinders
ssible.

The widespread development of radio in the 1920s, espe-
lly with some key Canadian inventions, made it one of the
rnerstones of modern mass media. Cheap newspapers and
ıgazines, radio networks, movies with sound, repeat adver-
ing, and instant communication by telephone were new cul-
al realities.

During those early decades of the 20th century, the
lantic Ocean delayed the distribution of information, prod-
ts, technology, and fads from overseas. At the same time,
l and truck transportation fostered economic and social ties
tween Canada and the United States. The U.S. rapidly
olaced England as the main source of Canadian social,
tertainment, and fashion influences.

Many attempts were made over the years to lessen the
pact of American cultural influences and to nurture a
ınadian cultural industry. Government-owned national broad-
sting networks, the Canadian Radio Broadcasting
ommission (now the CBC), and Radio-Canada, were created
ring the 1930s and began TV broadcasting in the 1950s. In
e 1960s, the Canadian Radio-television Telecommunication

Commission (CRTC) imposed Canadian content regulations
for radio and television, a move that revitalized the Canadian
music and independent TV production industries. The
Canadian film industry was given special tax benefits in the
1970s.

By late in the 20th century, technological developments,
especially in computers, communications, and even biology,
had affected how we talked to one another, the games we
played, the way we received news and information, and even
how we perceived the creation of life and the universe. The
Internet, cell phones, Nintendo, GameBoy, CNN, genetic
engineering, and hundreds of other changes melted international cultural borders and strongly influenced expressions of
popular culture.

Looking at ourselves and our history through popular culture does not necessarily help us to understand the great and
monumental events that have made Canada what it is today.
But it does allow us to observe how Canadians have lived and
evolved as a people and as a nation within our increasingly
global society.

Popular culture is an extensive, multi-faceted topic,
impossible to cover completely in one publication. However,
students will find that many important individuals, groups,
and cultural issues are covered, from different perspectives, in
other books in this series.

Miriam Bardswich and Gerry Campbell

The following themes in popular culture have been developed through the images and primary documents found
in this book:

- Advertising, fashion, self-image, and status
- Celebrating Canada and Canadian achievements
- Evolution of mass media and media issues
  (e.g. Canadian content, impact of new technologies,
  violence, censorship)
- Gender and minority portrayal
- Mass market sports and entertainment
- Outside influences on Canadian culture
- Point of view: bias, stereotyping, objectivity
- Popular heroes

CANADIANS GREETED THE 20TH CENTURY with enthusiasm, by ringing church and fire bells, blowing whistles, firing 99-gun salutes, and lighting bonfires along the U.S. border. Canada was still a small, rural country of just 5.4 million people — "a British backwater." But growth, prosperity, increased technology and urbanization, and especially optimism were very evident. Popular culture reflected both the old and the new Canada.

As in the past, the wealthy attended military or debutante balls, elaborate house parties and opening nights at the theatre, travelled to fashionable resorts, and took steamboat cruises. They played tennis, golf, badminton, cricket and polo, and took up the newly popular game of curling.

The less wealthy attended church socials, enjoyed bandstand music in parks, went on picnics or to the beach, and relied on homemade entertainment. Men often frequented the saloons, although prohibitionists sought to change the "culture of work and drink." Favourite sports were lacrosse, hockey, football, baseball, boxing and, in the West, rodeo. Women, although considered "too delicate" for many physical pursuits, were also sports enthusiasts, both as players and as spectators.

The affordable bicycle was changing many leisure pursuits and breaking down social barriers along with some of the more strict moral standards. Although these were the days before radio, some people did have gramophones on which they could play the most recent recordings. In the cities, vaudeville shows were popular, as were music festivals, classical music societies, and a new Canadian invention, five-pin bowling. There was a rapid growth in the number of movie theatres. Many people still attended Chautauqua productions, events that were "part revival meeting and part vaudeville" featuring speakers, bands and glee clubs, plays, debates and discussions of current issues, books, and science. Most cities and towns had competing newspapers and new libraries. For many, however, the most important book, next to the Bible, was the "wish book" — the Eaton's, Simpson's, or Dupuis Frères catalogues.

World War I affected popular culture as it did all aspects of life. This was seen particularly in music. Although many of the most popular songs were British or American, Canadians wrote and published hundreds of songs. Military shows by groups such as *The Dumbells* toured the country to raise money for Victory Bonds, and entertained the troops overseas. Posters, magazine covers, advertisements, even toys bore a distinctly patriotic flavour. The "snapshot craze" was just beginning and allowed average soldiers, for the first time in history, to carry pictures of their loved ones to war.

fads

- Crayola crayons, crossword puzzles
- Chiclets, gumballs, LifeSavers (all new)
- Foxtrot, Turkey Trot, the "naughty" tango
- Jell-o, Oreo cookies
- Nickelodeon movie pictures
- Tobogganing, sleigh rides

CHIEF POP GUN

18-228. "Chief" Lever Action Pop Gun, shoots a cork, makes lots of noise, perfectly harmless, length 15 inches. Price...

▲ A popular toy sold in the **Eaton's Catalogue**, Fall & Winter, 1915-16.

◄ **Simpson's Catalog[ue]** Fall/Winter 1917-18. Fashions clearly chang[ed] throughout the decade[.] What was flaunted in one period may be completely unaccepta[ble] in another.

(Hudson's Bay Company Corporate Collection)

The Delightful Pastime of Tobogganing

"...The thrill of excitement as the toboggan gathers momentum, the invigorating swish through the keen air, the breathless negotiation of the various jumps...and the peaceful easing up the bottom, combine to give a kaleidoscopic enjoyment that is lacking in other pastimes... Long may the hold remain to add to the many other winter amusements which make Canada an object of envy to those in other climes who are denied similar pleasures..."

— *Maclean's*, 1908

1904
 movie theatre (Canadian concept)
opens in Brantford, Ontario

1906
25 Dec: First public radio broadcast by
inventor Quebecer Reginald Fessenden

1907
20 Nov: McLaughlin Motor Company
founded in Oshawa, Ontario

1900 – 1919

SPEED OF AUTOS 7 MILES PER HOUR

The speed at which automobiles shall be allowed to run in city streets caused an earnest discussion in the Municipal Committee of the Legislature today. Mr. Preston's bill would permit the machine to run at 10 miles an hour in any city, town, or village, and 15 miles an hour in the country...

Mr. Gibson pointed out that this was legislation for a limited class... "These people just drive their machines to show off," said he, "to see how fast they can go and how many people they can get to look at them..."

— *Toronto Daily Star*, 20 May 1903

(Glenbow Archives na-1328-1259)

...ys of Driving

Early automobile advertisement. ▶ Picnicking near Edmonton, 1913. The "Horseless Carriage" may have been a status symbol, but driving was not always a joy in the early 20th century. How was one to start a ...r without the hand crank kicking back? How *did* one drive? People ...ually learned by trial and error. And that trip to the country required ...e to pack more than a picnic basket. For a start, it was necessary to ...ke one or two spare tires, inner tubes, a tire pump, jack, chains, tow ...e, lantern, spare grease cup, and a crowbar for removing rocks on the ...d. Getting stranded for hours was not unusual if the car broke down, ...t stuck in a ditch, or bogged down on muddy roads.

Christmas Cards

The custom of exchanging Christmas cards began in Victorian England, making its way to North America in the late 1870s. The original "cards" were actually three-panel sheets of stationery, often showing family scenes. By the early 1900s, the above Christmas postcards, with both religious and secular themes, had become popular.

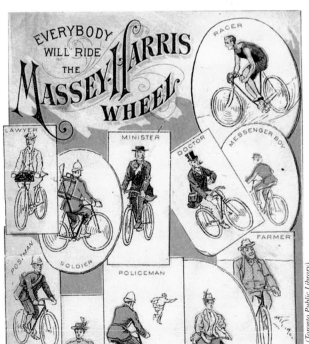

(Toronto Public Library)

▲ **The Bicycle Craze** The affordable bicycle was considered one of the most exciting inventions of the turn of the century. It offered mobility and a sense of freedom. People joined cycling clubs, entered races, and rode bicycles "built for two." Even women's fashions changed: "bloomers" were much more practical than full skirts for cycling.

1907
Deluxe movie theatre with
1 000 seats opens in Montreal

1909
Five-pin bowling invented by
Thomas Ryan of Toronto

1909
Dec: University of Toronto
wins first Grey Cup game

▲ **Hockey** was already "Canada's Sport" at the beginning of the 20th century. In 1900, top amateur hockey players were paid $200 for an eight-game season. There were seven players instead of six, and all played the entire game. It was played on a natural ice surface until the first artificial ice rinks opened in Victoria and Vancouver in 1912.

The National Hockey League (NHL), was created in 1917, an indica╵ that sports were becoming more commercial even before radio, la╵ stadiums, and indoor arenas. Pictures above show men's and wome╵ hockey teams, circa 1900.

◄ **Tommy Burns,** born Noah Brussc╵ was Canada's only heavyweight box╵ champion. He won the title in 1906 a╵ successfully defended it ten times. His knock-out of Irish champion, Jen╵ Roche, was the shortest defence ev╵ over in 1 minute, 28 seconds.

James Naismith: Inventor of Basketball

Basketball may have been introduced in the United States but the inventor, James Naismith, was Canadian. In December 1891 Naismith, himself an outstanding athlete in lacrosse and rugby, was asked to devise an indoor game for winter. Using a soccer ball and half bushel peach baskets, the new game was played on the gym floor. In 1912 the bottoms were cut out of the baskets, and later baskets were replaced with hoops. By 1900, there were professional leagues and basketball was an exhibition sport in the 1904 Olympics.

▲ **Tom Longboat** of the Six Nations Reserve in Brantford, Ontario, was one of most widely celebrated athletes of the early 20th century. Pictured above with his trophy for the 1907 Boston Marathon, he also won the World Marathon Championship in 1909, breaking numerous records. He would continue racing during World War I, as a dispatch runner in France.

(NAC C 014094)

1910	1912	1912	1912
7 Aug: Thomas Edison synchronizes pictures with sound in film	2 Sept: First Calgary Stampede	Stephen Leacock's *Sketches of a Little Town* published	Quebec vaudeville star Eva Tanguay becomes highest paid actress in America

1900 – 1919

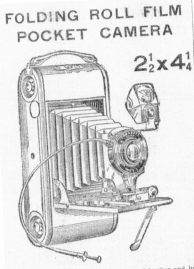

◄ **The Camera** was starting to be used as a tool for artistic expression. In this 1905 picture, *Fantasy (portrait of a woman with an oriental mask),* by Sidney Carter, the focus has been manipulated to create a work of art, rather than just a copy of the subject.

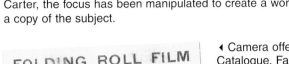

◄ Camera offered for sale in the Eaton's Catalogue, Fall & Winter, 1916-17. While the professional portrait was expensive for working class families, people were fascinated with the camera and the "snapshot craze" was just beginning. The first box camera had been invented in 1888 by Kodak and would gradually become more affordable.

▼ Children of Cape Breton coal miner pose for a portrait, circa 1919.

(Courtesy N. Liutkus)

The Royal Muskoka Hotel was one of over 30 built in the Muskoka Lakes area of Ontario before 1880 and was popular with wealthy tourists at the turn of the century. These resorts were complete with ballrooms, formal dining rooms, tennis courts, croquet lawns, and luxury accommodation. There were also resort hotels in the mountains of British Columbia and by the sea in New Brunswick and Nova Scotia.

Proper Bathing Attire A regatta day in front of Hanlan's Point Hotel on Toronto Island. Hanlan's Point was named after the Hanlan family who settled here in the 1860s. The most famous member of the family was Ned Hanlan who gained international recognition for his success in rowing during the late 19th century.

(City of Toronto, Fonds 1244, Item 163)

"I'm too homely for a prima donna and too ugly for a soubrette."

▸ **Marie Dressler**, in *Dinner at Eight*, 1933. Born in Coburg, Ontario, Marie Dressler was a vaudeville and musical comedy star. In 1914 she made her screen debut as Charlie Chaplin's co-star in Tillie's *Punctured Romance*. In 1930 she would win an Academy Award for best actress in *Min and Bill*.

MARIE DRESSLER APPEARS TONIGHT

Funniest Woman on English-Speaking Stage
Will Be Headliner at Last Arena Concert

The great festival at the Arena…will feature…Miss Marie Dressler… It is the aim of Miss Dressler to give the public something of a higher order than mere burlesque…though it is not generally known [she is] a most thoroughly trained musician, familiar with every detail of her art… It is this musical training that enables her to so skilfully satirize the prima donnas of the day….

— *Toronto World,* 12 October 1912

▲ **Louis B. Mayer** was an immigrant child from New Brunswick who "made it big" in Hollywood. In 1916 he founded his own production company which would become MGM in 1924. He produced such hit movies as *Ben Hur*, *Dinner at Eight*, and *Grand Hotel*. To many, he was one of the most powerful figures in Hollywood.

(NLC)

The World wasn't made in a day,
And Eve didn't ride on a bus,
But most of the earth's in a sandbag,
The rest of it's plastered on us

— From the *Wipers Times,* 12 February 1916 and cited in *The Communication Trench* by Will R. Bird

◂ **Music of the Great War** Hundreds of pieces of Canadian sheet music were printed during the war. Colourful and with catchy titles, they were clea[rly] patriotic. There was also a strong British influence with songs such as "Bles[s] 'em All," "Lillie Marlene," "Now is the Hour," and "Pack Up Your Troubles."

1917
26 Nov: National Hockey League (NHL) formed

1918
1 Apr: Federal government introduces Prohibition

1919
Dec: XWA (later CFCF) begins broadcasting — thought to be oldest radio station in the world

1900 – 1919

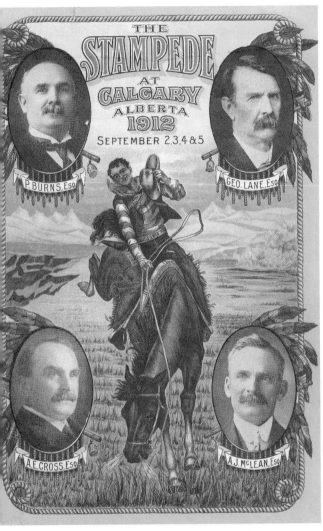

The Calgary Stampede was organized in 1912 by Guy Weadick and financed by the "Big Four Cattlemen" featured in the above poster. They put up $100 000, hoping the fair and rodeo would help promote the depressed cattle industry.

Flores La Due, or Mrs. Weadick, was a star attraction at her husband's stampede. She was the "World Champion Fancy Roper." She is shown here in 1912.

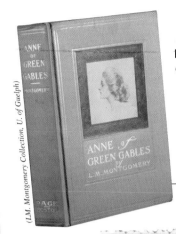

(L.M. Montgomery Collection, U. of Guelph)

◀ **Anne of Green Gables** by Lucy Maud Montgomery (picture shows cover of first edition) was an instant success when it was published in 1908. The story of the "plucky redhead" has continued to delight generations of young girls. It enjoys worldwide popularity in countries as diverse as the United States and Japan.

THE CREMATION OF SAM MCGEE

…There wasn't a breath in that land of death,
And I hurried, horror-driven,
With a corpse half hid that I couldn't get rid,
Because of a promise given;
It was lashed to the sleigh, and it seemed to
Say: 'You may tax your brawn and brains,
But you promised true, and it's up to you to
Cremate those last remains.'…

▲ **Robert Service's** lengthy poem, written while in the Klondike, was published in *Songs of the Sourdough* (1907). In the poem, "Sam McGee," a Tennessee prospector in the Yukon, fearing that his end was near, asked his fellow prospector to cremate his last remains. Coming upon a derelict ship, his buddy starts a fire in the boiler to cremate Sam. Immensely popular in Canada, the United States, and even Europe, Service was known as "the Poet of the Yukon" and "the Canadian Kipling." To his readers, the Yukon was as Service depicted it.

(McMaster University Archives)

The Song My Paddle Sings

West wind blow from your prairie nest
Blow from the mountains,
blow from the west,
the sail is idle, the sailor too;
O! Wind of the west, we wait for you.

◀ "The Song My Paddle Sings" was first recited by Anglo-native poet **Pauline Johnson**, or Tekahionwake, in 1892. Her first collection of poetry, *White Wampum* was published in 1895. During a series of Canadian, American, and British tours between 1892 and 1910, Pauline Johnson came to be regarded as a strong nationalist, a "cultural ambassador" for Canada.

WHEN THE YOUTH OF THE 1920S were children, two cataclysmic events occurred: World War I had taken the lives of 16 million people and left millions of others maimed; and the great flu epidemic of 1919 took another 20 million lives worldwide. There were very few families in Europe or North America who had not lost at least one relative, friend, or neighbour in those tragedies. This might explain why "the Lost Generation" has become known as one of the wildest generations in the 20th century.

North American urban popular culture reflects a generation that loved to buy, to dance, to dress in sexually provocative clothes, to drink, to collect luxuries, and generally to live "the high life." Cole Porter set his smash musical, *Anything Goes*, which featured the hit tune "I Get a Kick Out of You," in this era.

The sentimental parlour music of previous decades was drowned out by gramophone records that featured revolutionary and scandalous jazz. Thus, one name given to this wild decade was "the Jazz Age." But jazz was not the only musical influence. Brazilian and other Latin music had a significant impact, as did new dance forms such as the Charleston.

By the late 1920s, the film industry had become very successful. A few of its superstars, such as Canadian Mary Pickford, moved from acting to film producing and promoting, accumulating enormous wealth and status. Their influence spread to fashion as young women switched from the completely modest clothing styles of the previous generation to the high heels, silk stockings, and very short skirts of the "flapper."

The wild, devil-may-care attitude of the "Roaring Twenties" was fuelled by rapid changes in technology. The automobile allowed people to travel much more widely and impetuously than the horse and buggy of their parents' era. The telephone and radio revolutionized communication, marketing, tastes, and lifestyles. Millions attended movies and flocked to the "talkies" as soon as they were introduced. Despite Prohibition, the sale and consumption of illegal alcohol was widespread, supporting an underworld of "speakeasies," gambling, and other organized criminal activities. Criminals became heroes and legends in the popular press, movies, and pulp fiction. With all that excitement and bad alcohol, another invention, the painkiller, became so common that the decade also became known as "the Aspirin Age."

The high-flying excesses came to a sudden halt in 1929 with the collapse of the stock market and the beginnings of the Great Depression. The wild times of the 1920s went out with a bang.

fads

- The Charleston
- Crossword puzzles, jigsaw puzzles, Mah-Jongg
- Raccoon skin coats
- Wide-cut pants
- The little black dress
- Home movie cameras / projectors
- Popsicles, bubblegum, Kool-Aid
- Hardy Boys books
- Yo-Yo's

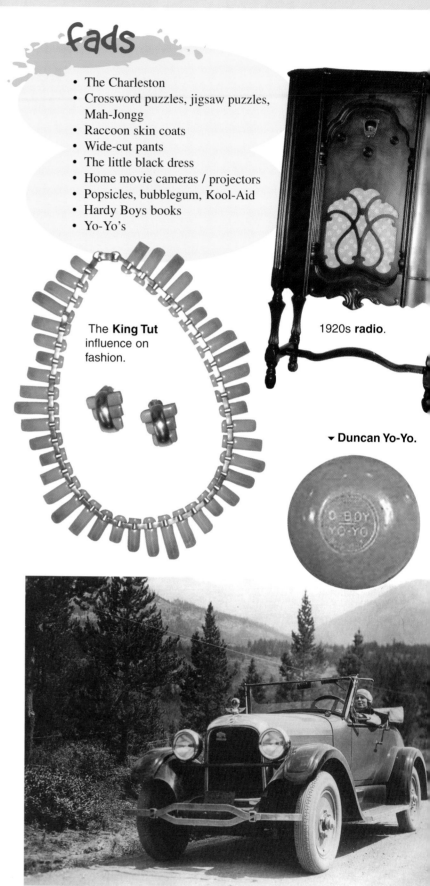

The **King Tut** influence on fashion.

1920s **radio**.

▼ **Duncan Yo-Yo.**

▲ **The automobile** represented freedom, independence, and status. Gas pow vehicles, tractors, and other equipment were changing work patterns and leisu time activities: faster deliveries; less manual work on farms; urbanization, crea of the suburb, driving to "the game" or to pick up one's date.

1922	1923	1924	1927
radio stations in Canada	Famous Players of Hollywood takes over leading Canadian cinema chain	Canadians invent synchronized swimming	Mazo de la Roche's *Jalna* becomes best-seller

1920
–
1929

Ethel **Smith** (left) and **Fanny "Bobbie" Rosenfeld** (right) in the women's 100m dash at the 1928 Olympic Games in Amsterdam.

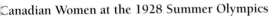

Canadian Women at the 1928 Summer Olympics

This year in Amsterdam, Holland, for the first time in athletic history, women athletes were given an official and definitive place on an Olympic program. That they made good beyond all shadow of doubt is admired wherever there are broadminded sportsmen… And they won the world's track and field championship… Six girls from Canada…were pitted against…a total of 121 competitors…. And when the last race was won, the unofficial score stood: Canada 26, United States 20, Germany 18 with the rest trailing nowhere near the leaders….

— *Maclean's*, October 1928

(*Glenbow Archives na-352-1*)

▲ **The Edmonton Grads** amateur basketball team was the most successful team, male or female, amateur or professional, in Canadian history. They lost only 20 games out of 522 between 1915-40. In the 1924 Olympics they played and won 27 games against Europeans. They wore "heavy woollen stockings…voluminous knee-length bloomers (made of three yards of British serge)" topped with long team sweaters.

"You are not only an inspiration to basketball players throughout the world, but a model of all girls' teams. Your attitude and success have been a source of gratification to me in illustrating the possibilities of the game in the development of the highest type of womanhood."

— James Naismith (inventor of basketball) to the Grads, 1936

Hewitt in a fog in radio debut — 23 March 1923

The Star had just purchased CFCA, the first radio station in Toronto and Lake, after failing to find any senior staff willing to accept the task, told Hewitt he would be calling that night's hockey game… Hewitt called the game over a phone but the real problem turned out to be seeing the game he was supposed to be calling… "I had to keep calling and wiping the glass at the same time," Hewitt said… "I even had to leave the mike and go outside and keep wiping so I could see what was going on."… The mike, which was actually a phone, also caused problems… "Every once in awhile the operator would come on the line and ask what number you were calling and it would go off the air," Hewitt told the *Globe and Mail's* Blair Kirby on the 50th anniversary of the broadcast….

— *Toronto Sun*, 6 December 1999

"He shoots!... he scores!"

Foster Hewitt: "Play by Play" hockey announcer.

(Provincial Archives of Alberta)

(Glenbow Archives na-2273-5)

◂ **Cowboys at the Calgary Stamped** 1923. At this event, the rodeo was bro back, the famous chuck wagon races were introduced, and a record attenda figure of 138 950 was achieved. The mayor, businessmen, and average cit all became cowboys and cowgirls for duration of the Stampede.

The Calgary Stampede with its wo derful success has brought back th old Calgary spirit more than anyth else... [It's] phenomenal success... revived the old spirit of confidence the old community spirit...

— *The Albertan*, July 1923

◂ **Vaudeville** was the main form of public entertainment until movies became popular. Performers included singers, comedians, performing dogs, tricks on bicycles, jugglers, and other acts.

▸ **Mary Pickford** From "Moppet" to "America's Sweetheart" to "Mogul," Toronto-born Mary Pickford became famous for her film work long before World War I though she is usually identified as "a star of the twenties." With Charlie Chaplin, her former boss D.W. Griffith, and her husband Douglas Fairbanks, Mary would help found United Artist Studio in 1919. Pickford was one of the first movie "stars" and one of the first actors to take control of her own career and image. Hollywood may have started to influence Canadian popular culture but Canadians were helping to shape Hollywood.

"No — I really cannot afford to work for only ten thousand a week."

— Mary Pickford, to Adolph Zukor, 1916

"Bank of America's Sweetheart."

— Charlie Chaplin, describing Pickford, 1916

...[T]he box office value of every star who appears to advantage on the air is greatly enhanced, and, potentially speaking, so is the stock of the company to which he or she is under contract.

So far as competition to pictures is concerned, that I view as a boon. Competition always has been, always will be, the greater incentive to better effort.

...The great disadvantage of the radio, however, is that it does not gratify the individual's gregarious urge. No one likes to sit constantly at home... The essence of entertainment is variety. And what variety is there for the housewife, who has been at home all day, in sitting down amid the same surroundings to listen even to the most divine symphony or the most romantic love story ever told...

— Mary Pickford, 1934, on the future of radio and possibly television

LOVE STORIES FROM THE MOVIES

ScreenBook *Magazine*

25 Cents

Mary Pickfor

Coquette

The Full-Length Story Complete in this Issue

Also Complete Stories of

The Trial of Mary Dugan

The Desert Song···Leatherneck

The fashions of today have never been so sane. Take the length of the average skirt, the comfortable neck, the freedom of the sleeve which all tend toward health and happiness. They are a reflection of the occupations and enjoyment of the people of today.

— *Toronto Star*, 1922

A FLAPPER'S APPEAL TO PARENTS

If one judge by appearances, I suppose I am a flapper. I am within the age limit. I wear bobbed hair...I powder my nose. I wear fringe skirts and bright-coloured sweaters, and scarfs, and shirts with Peter Pan collars, and low-heeled "finale hopper" shoes. I adore to dance. I spend a large amount of time in automobiles. I attend hops, and proms, and ball-games...

Oh, parents, parents everywhere, point out to us the ideals of truly glorious and upright living! Believe in us, that we may learn to believe in ourselves...

We are the Younger Generation. The war tore away our spiritual foundations and challenges our faith. We are struggling to regain our equilibrium. The times have made us older and more experienced than you were at our age. It must be so with each succeeding generation if it is to keep pace with the rapidly advancing and mighty tide of civilization...

— Ellen Welles Page in *Outlook Magazine*, 6 December 1922

"Cranks throughout the country go around and ask why the Liquor Act is not being enforced. I say that in its present state it is impossible to enforce it... [T]here's lots of liquor and there's lots of drinking. And, it's the worse kind of drinking — canned heat and wood alcohol..."

— Calgary Magistrate, Col. G. E. Sanders, December 1921

▲ **Defying Prohibition** A flapper shows how a bottle of liquor can be smuggled in her garter.

(Glenbow Archives na-3217-2)

▲ Police officers from Alberta pose with a confiscated still.

(Glenbow Archives na-2890-13)

1930
Canada's first talking movie
The Vikings filmed

1931
Maple Leaf Gardens
opens in Toronto

THE GREAT DEPRESSION reduced Canadians to desperation and this was reflected in a popular culture that railed against misfortune and sought to escape it. Perhaps nothing reflects the unemployment and hardships of the period better than John Steinbeck's 1939 novel, *The Grapes of Wrath,* and Yip Harburg's lyrics in "Brother Can You Spare a Dime?" Although both were American, Canadians could easily identify with the plight of farmers who lost their land in the "Dust Bowl" and with the misfortunes of unemployed World War I veterans.

While music was often sad to reflect the times, it ran the gamut of emotions, from Louis Armstrong's bittersweet "All of Me," to "I Don't Want Your Millions Mister," to Duke Ellington's "It Don't Mean a Thing if it Ain't Got That Swing." The Swing Era of big band jazz packed dance halls across the continent. As well, Canadians listened to the music of Canada's Guy Lombardo and other top American bands on live radio broadcasts.

Radio shows, movies, cheap novels, and magazine fiction provided further escape. Many popular radio shows, *Abbot and Costello, The Lone Ranger, Jack Benny, Truth or Consequences,* and afternoon "soap operas" came from the U.S. To counter that influence, the government established a Canadian public network in 1932. By the end of the decade, CBC and Radio Canada shows such as *Hockey Night in Canada, The Happy Gang, Just Mary Stories* for children, and any show about "the royals" were capturing the biggest audiences.

Movies offered fantasy with *Mickey Mouse, Snow White,* and other Disney animations, chills with *Frankenstein* and *Dracula,* opulent Busby Berkley musicals, and romance with movies such as *Gone With the Wind.* Among the great stars were many Canadians including Beatrice Lillie and Marie Dressler in comedy, Fay Wray of *King King* fame, Deanna Durbin, Raymond Massey, Walter Huston, and Donald Woods. While Hollywood dominated the movie industry, efforts were being made to create a Canadian film industry to produce documentaries that would "interpret Canada and Canadians to other countries." To this end, the National Film Board was established in 1939.

The ultimate popular escapism was the fascination with images of innocence exemplified by little girls. The royal princesses, Elizabeth and Margaret, were constantly in the news. The "darling moppet" of American movies was Shirley Temple and little girls everywhere dreamed of having her doll. And in Canada the Dionne Quintuplets, exploited by business and the Ontario government, were made a tourist attraction. Millions travelled to Callander, Ontario to view the Quints at play in a special compound.

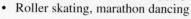

fads

- Baseball cards sold with chewing gum
- Board games, e.g. the new Monopoly
- Card games, especially Bridge
- Kraft macaroni and cheese
- "Knock knock" jokes
- Table top tennis, miniature golf
- Knickerbockers, Oxford baggy pants look for men
- Roller skating, marathon dancing

▸ Colourful **Depression glass**, often given away as a marketing promotion. Many are now valuable collectibles.

▸ The **Superman** character was created by Toronto-born artist Joe Shuster and Cleveland writer Jerry Siegel in 1933 and given its own comic in 1939. Mild-mannered Clark Kent worked for the *Daily Star,* modelled after the *Toronto Star,* although the paper's name would later be changed to *The Daily Planet.* The first Superman movie appeared in 1948 and the TV show in 1953. In a 1978 version of the movie, Lois Lane would be played by Canadian actor Margot Kidder. The first edition cover of the comic book (shown here) sold for $51 750 in 1999.

(Glenbow Archives na-4868-212)

◂ **Grey Owl**, alias Archie Belaney, was a noted conservationist and writer who claimed to be the son of a Scot and an Apache. His books, including *The Men of the Last Frontier* (his first, published in 1931) *Pilgrims of the Wild* (1934), and others were widely acclaimed. It was not until his death in 1938 that it was discovered that he was actually an Englishman.

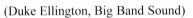

◂ **Wilf Carter** (1932), singer and songwriter from Nova Scotia, became a cowboy when he moved to Alberta. Two of his radio hits were "My Swiss Moonlight Lullaby" and "The Capture of Albert Johnson." He also recorded in the U.S. where his stage name was "Montana Slim."

"It Don't Mean a Thing if it Ain't Got That Swing"

(Duke Ellington, Big Band Sound)

— Duke Ellington was just one of the big band leaders to play Canadian venues. Count Basie, Tommy Dorsey, Mart Kenney, Guy Lombardo and His Royal Canadians all played here. People flocked to the dance hall pavilions from the mid-thirties and throughout the forties.

Brother, Can You Spare a Dime

(Gorney/Harburg)

…

Once I built a railroad, I made it run,
Made it race against time.
Once I built a railroad; now it's done.
Brother, can you spare a dime?

— Called "the most poignant anthem of the Depression," this song captures the spirit of the decade through the words of a World War I soldier who is reduced to begging.

Skate-sailing on the pond.

"Shirley Temple. That's what I remember about the Thirties. Shirley Temple Dolls… I'd stand there and watch the faces of those little girls, from about four or five right up to eleven… Little faces, they needed food. You could see a lot who needed a pint of milk a day a thousand times more than they needed a Shirley doll. They'd stare for hours… The kids weren't the only ones, but, the mothers too, and the hopeless look on their faces and trying to shush the little girls away, knowing they only had a dollar or two to buy gifts for the whole family… I wonder if Shirley Temple ever realized the misery that those dolls must have caused…"

— From a female clerk in Eaton's toy department, cited in *Colombo's Book of Canada*

1930 – 1939

SIMPSON'S CanadaWide

CANADIAN SCHOONER "BLUENOSE" CHAMPION OF THE NORTH ATLANTIC FISHING FLEETS

Fall 1932 Number
SEND YOUR ORDERS TO TORONTO

(Hudson's Bay Company Corporate Collection)

▴ **The Bluenose** (here on the cover of a Simpson's Catalogue) was a fishing schooner from Lunenburg, Nova Scotia. It was famous for its racing ability, winning the International Fishermen's Trophy throughout the 1920s and '30s. Since 1937 it has appeared on the Canadian dime.

HOCKEY KEPT UP DURING LAST WAR

Stanley Cup Playoffs Between East, West and Allan Cup Championship Rounds Continues (Montreal Sept. 3)

Possibility that some of Canada's major sports events may be curtailed, if not abandoned altogether because of war, was seen tonight by leading athletic figures.

— *Globe and Mail*, 4 September 1939

GENERAL MOTORS HOCKEY BROADCAST NEWS

GM HOCKEY BROADCASTS HANG UP NEW HIGH MARKS IN QUALITY AND COVERAGE

Listening Audience Grows From Thousands to Millions In Three Winters

---

…Majority Not Sport Followers But Look on Hockey as Gripping Drama

(CBC Archives)

◄ **The Happy Gang** was Canada's longest running radio show (1937-59). Noted for its corny jokes and spontaneity, the show was recorded in front of a live audience. It regularl showcased stars such as Oscar Peterson and introduced new Canadian talent.

The Dionne Quintuplets

They were taken from their parents by the Ontario government shortly after their birth. The Quints became a "$500 million dollar asset" to the Ontario government during the Depression. They were put on display at a Quint theme park. There were also radio appearances, story, colouring and cutout books, souvenirs, and dolls. In 1998 Ontario agreed to pay the three surviving Dionnes $4 million in compensation.

There's Gold i "Them Thar Quin

— *Toronto Star Weekly,* 22 August 1936

Corbeil's Famed Babes Greatest Tourist Lure In Province's History

Dionne Infants Attracted More Than 250,000 Visitors in 1935; Influx in Approaching Summer Is Expected to Exceed 500,000

ADVERTISED BY ALL TOURIST, TRAVEL BUREAUS

◄ Quintland.　　　　▲ The Quints perform on CBC Radio, 193

1939
Royal Winnipeg
Ballet founded

1939
2 Mar: National Film
Board founded

1939
30 Apr: Television
debuts at World Fair

1939
10 Sept: Canada enters World War II
by declaring war on Germany

ay Wray, an Alberta-born actor, made
eral silent films in the 1920s and then
ed to "talkies." She is best known for
role as Ann Darrow in the horror
ie *King Kong*, made in 1933.

apitol Records, 1939.

1930 – 1939

ourity of mind, unthinking loyalty and marital happiness can be secured by
isorship, then Canadians should possess those qualities in a high degree...
here have been two recent examples... One was the banning of the maga-
e *Ken* for a cartoon about George VI and his suggested visit to the World's
r... The other example was the refusal of the Quebec Film Board, to allow
e showing of *Wuthering Heights*, on the ground that it portrayed 'infidelity.'

"Canadian Censorship," *The Canadian Forum*, June 1939

"The morals of yesterday are no more.
hey are as dead as the day they were
ived. Economic independence has put
women on the same footing as men."
— Norma Shearer

Norma Shearer in *Satin Ladies*, 1935. Originally from Montreal, she was one of the
mour queens of the 1930s and she was considered by some to be "queen of the
" During this decade she starred in historical films such as *Romeo and Juliet* and
rie Antoinette, and made several escapist movies.

"Every picture of merit made since
the Depression engulfed us has met
with financial success in spite of trying
economic conditions and drastic criticism aimed at the industry from many
quarters.... The outstanding popularity
of Will Rogers, Janet Gaynor and little
Shirley Temple indicates that the world
wants simple, human screen fare, fundamental in emotion and wholesome
in motivation."

— Mary Pickford, 1934

1940 - 1949

WORLD WAR II WAS THE DOMINANT influence on popular culture in the first half of the 1940s. In military bases and across the country, shows kept up spirits. Three of the most popular were *The Army Show*, whose skits were written and performed by Sergeants Johnny Wayne and Frank Shuster, *Rodeo Rhythm*, and *Meet the Navy*.

Pictures of American pin-up girls and Canada's "Bren Gun Girl" decorated barracks and planes. Posters, bubble gum cards, colouring books, Christmas cards, magazines, and milk bottle tops, all featured military and patriotic themes. Hollywood also went to war with many patriotic films, among them *Casablanca* and *The Flight Lieutenant* starring Canadian-born Glenn Ford.

People devoured newspaper accounts of the war and attended movies almost as much for the newsreels as for the movies themselves. Wartime radio presented dramatic real-life stories, vivid newscasts, and soap operas such as "Soldier's Wife." Magazines such as *Maclean's* printed fictional short stories. This was also "the Golden Age of Canadian Comics" with Canadian action heroes defeating the Nazis and Japanese in every issue.

World War I songs became popular again, as did songs from Britain. Big bands remained popular and dance pavilions were packed with soldiers and sailors on leave. One of the most popular songs was Frank Sinatra's "I'll Never Smile Again" by Toronto songwriter Ruth Lowe. "White Christmas," recorded by Bing Crosby in 1942, marked the real beginning of secular Christmas music and has become the best-selling song of all time.

With the end of war came celebrations and a return to peacetime pursuits. Women left their wartime jobs and returned to the home. The military look in women's fashion was traded in for elegance and femininity. The "bikini," named after the tiny Pacific island of Bikini where the Americans tested the atomic bomb, caused a sensation. It was banned on public beaches in Canada. In Quebec, women were fined for wearing short shorts.

Heroes were now found in entertainment, on the playing field, and on the ice rink. Teenage girls swooned over crooner Frank Sinatra. Canadian girls took up figure skating after Barbara Ann Scott won the 1947 World Figure Skating title and the 1948 Olympic gold medal. The popular *Hockey Night in Canada* broadcast the play-by-play of five Stanley Cups for the Toronto Maple Leafs during the decade. In the West, football fever raged.

During the war and immediately following it, Canadians turned to CBC and Radio-Canada. But television was on its way as American stations began broadcasting across the border.

fads

- Comic book craze
- "Cutting In" or "Excuse Me" dances
- Jitterbugging
- Goldfish swallowing
- Pin-ups — Betty Grable, Rita Hayworth, Veronica Lake, Jane Russell

▲ The **"zoot sooters"** were young men who rebelled against wartime clothing restrictions and society in general by wearing outrageous clothes.

Shots Fired, 400 Sailors Drag Zoot Suiters to Battle

Zoot Suit Battle Brings Murder Attempt Case

MONTREAL CLUB BANS ZOOTERS

…Naval authorities declared there will be a federal investigation into the rio which have forced provincial, city and service police to maintain emergen schedules for several days.… Police laid the blame for the start of the figh "on both sides." Sailors, they said, reported the "copiously clothed zoot-sui ers flaunted their extra yards of material" in front of them.

"They are defiance suits," said one sailor. "When other civilians could get cuffs on their trousers yards of material were going into 'drape shapes,' ar most of the ones wearing them do nothing but hang around poolrooms…"

— *Toronto Daily Star,* 5 June 1944

1941

IFB documentary *Churchill's Island* about Battle of Britain becomes first Canadian film to win an Oscar

1942

Disney's animated cartoon *Bambi* is family hit

1943

Wayne and Shuster star in *The Army Show* — Saskatchewan farmer Kit Carson directs western version of the show, *Rodeo Rhythm*

When **Barbara Ann Scott** returned to Canada after winning the 1947 World Figure Skating championship she was greeted by thousands of fans and showered in presents. She returned the expensive gifts in order to keep her amateur status. After winning the Olympic gold medal in 1948 she turned professional.

(CP Photo/John J. Lent)

Montreal Negro Star Hitting .371 and Showing Flashy Form at Keystone

On 18 April 1946, Jackie Robinson, playing for the minor league Montreal Royals, broke the colour bar in American baseball. He would lead Montreal to the Little World Series and in 1947 join big league baseball with the Brooklyn Dodgers. He would endure racial slurs, even death threats during his baseball career but he and his wife would always retain fond memories of Montreal.

— *The Sporting News,* 21 August 1946

◄ **Jackie Robinson**, 1946.

1940 – 1949

(NAC C 143027)

Johnny Canuck was the archetypal symbol of the Canadian war effort. Strong, pure, handsome, and courageous, he was the nemesis of the Axis, fighting relentlessly in the cause of freedom.

— *The Great Canadian Comic Books*, 1971

The beautiful voice of Winnipeg-born **Deanna Durbin** and the new movie magazines helped people forget about the Depression, if only for a few minutes. At 15, Durbin was already a star with MGM.

▸ **Harlequin Romance**, founded in Winnipeg in 1949, is one of the most popular publishers of romance fiction in the world, selling in 131 countries and 25 languages. In a March 2003 interview with *Maclean's* magazine, Donna Hayes, CEO of Harlequin Enterprises, stated that the books are not written to formula but that "the one thing that is an absolute constant… is that there has to be a happy ending." Millions of readers have looked for exactly that. Image on the right shows cover of the first Harlequin Romance novel.

(Courtesy Harlequin)

▲ Soldiers and the **war effort** were featured in most publications throughout the war years.

♫ *Hit Songs of WW II* ♫

Boogie Woogie Bugle Boy (The Andrew Sisters)

Coming in on a Wing and a Prayer (The Song Spinners)

A Nightingale Sang in Berkeley Square (Vera Lynn)

Lili Marlene (A German hit "adopted" by the Allies)

Paper Doll (The Mills Brothers)

Spring Will Be a Little Late This Year (Deanna Durbin)

There'll Always Be an England

The White Cliffs of Dover (Vera Lynn)

▲ **Christmas letter** from Canadian soldier in Italy, 1944.

▲ Celebrating **Victory in Europe** (VE) Day, Toronto, 8 May 1945.

22

(Region of Peel Archives)

▲ Popular **songsheets**.

(Courtesy Donna Bardswich)

(CP Photo)

1940 – 1949

▲ **Guy Lombardo and His Royal Canadians**, which had taken the name "Royal Canadians" in 1924, was one of the most popular dance bands of the 1940s. They are best remembered for their New Year's Eve broadcasts, first on radio and later on television. Their New Year's Eve theme song, "Auld Lang Syne," has been wildly successful, selling over 300 million copies world wide.

WAYNE:	*"We can make a movie right here in Canada. Why go to Hollywood?"*
SHUSTER:	*"You're right John. Canada is the place."*
WAYNE:	*"Sure Hollywood. What's so great about Hollywood? You work, you slave, you kill yourself and at the end of the year, what have you got? A fortune."*

— Johnny Wayne and Frank Shuster, radio short, 1946

◄ **The "Bren Gun Girl"** Her name was Veronica "Ronnie" Foster and she worked on the Bren Gun production line in Toronto during WW II. Her picture became a favourite among Canadian soldiers. She's seen here jitterbugging at the Glen Eagle Country Club in Toronto, May 1941.

1950 - 1959

1950
"Cool Jazz"
becomes popular

1950
Howie Morenz and Bobbie Rosenfeld
are "Athletes of the Half-Century"

IT WAS KNOWN AS "The Fabulous Fifties," a decade that saw the first of the postwar baby boomer generation become teenagers and begin to define North American popular culture. People remember the 1950s as a period of affluence, a time when life was less stressful and much safer. Nostalgia glosses over the economic recession, regional disparities, the Cold War arms race, McCarthyism, the Korean Conflict, and the Hungarian Revolution.

By 1954, 22% of Canadian households had televisions; ten years later it would be close to 90%. Canadians watched American shows such as *Leave it to Beaver*, *Ed Sullivan*, and *American Bandstand*. They also watched homegrown shows such as *Juliette*, *The Friendly Giant*, *Les Plouffe* in English and French versions, and *Hockey Night in Canada*.

Like the times, television was quite conservative. It barely reflected the revolutionary cultural spirit that was being expressed in poetry, in drama, and especially in rock and roll. When Elvis Presley first appeared on the *Ed Sullivan Show*, he was shown only from the waist up. It was considered a bold move when CBC allowed deodorant ads. Nevertheless, television revolutionized how we viewed ourselves and others. TV brought news, entertainment, controversy, and advertising into our living rooms and fed our thirst for what was new.

The movie industry introduced 3-D, wider screens, and more films in colour to compete with black and white TV. For the young, Saturday afternoon Westerns and *The Three Stooges* were the rage — two movies, a "pop," and popcorn cost 25 cents.

This became "the teenage decade." Youth had purchasing power and their own preferences in movies, TV, magazines, cars, fashion, and music. They frequented drive-in movies, soda fountains, skating rinks, drive-in restaurants, or just cruised around in flashy cars with wide fins and lots of chrome. Worried about not having dates, teens thought "going steady" was the solution. School dress codes were still strict — no jeans, no T-shirts, no pants for girls. After school it was the James Dean/Marlon Brando "rebel" look with jeans rolled up over Wellington boots for boys; and poodle skirts, tapered plaid slacks, cardigans buttoned up the back, and penny loafers for girls.

However, music most clearly defined the decade. Rock and roll, progressive jazz, beat and folk music were exciting and liberating; and parents hated it. Elvis Presley, Little Richard, Buddy Holly, and others were the new teen idols. Canada produced its own stars: the *Crew Cuts*, *The Four Lads*, and Ottawa's Paul Anka with the hit song, "Diana."

While the musical form was new and radical, rock and roll lyrics did not deal with social or international issues. That came in the 1960s.

fads

- Rolled up jeans
- Poodle skirts, saddle shoes
- The Brando/Dean rebel look
- Ducktail, crewcut hairdos
- Ruby red lipstick
- Davy Crockett coonskin caps
- Monster bingo
- Cramming telephone booths
- Hula hoop, frisbee, LEGO
- TV dinners

▲ **The hula hoop** was an Australian invention that became one of North America's hottest fads in 1958. The g[irl] above twirls four hula hoops at once.

(Courtesy Cindy Fawcett, Owner Ric's Boardwalk Ice Cream Parlor)

▲ **1955 Seeburgh Juke Box**
At Ric's Boardwalk Ice Cream Parlour in Burlington, Ontario, you can still get two plays for 25¢. Ric's, originally half of the Old Victorian Restaurant, was frequented by stars such as Frank Sinatra, Marilyn Monroe and Fats Domino when Burlington was known as "The Las Vegas of the North." Today, it's like stepping back in time with old movie posters, 1950s memorabilia, and the original rock music.

"Slang"

Blast	A great time
Cool	Long drawn out "coooool"
Cool it	Settle down
Crazy	Especially good, "really cool"
Drag	A bore or a boring time
Flat-top	A crew cut, flat on the top
Gig	A job
Hang	As in "hang out"
Hep or Hip	Someone who is cool
Kick	A fun time, a fad
Later	As in "See ya later, alligator"
No sweat	No problem
Split	Leave
Unreal	Exceptional

'CAR CRAZINESS':
A MENACE TO OUR TEENAGERS?

Psychologists paint the gloomiest picture of all. Some of them warn that the teenager's car, as the chief symbol of soft living, may debase him mentally, physically, spiritually and morally to the point where, like the enervating public baths of ancient Rome, it leads to the decline and fall of the nation.

— *Maclean's*, 6 June 1959

♫ Top of the Charts ♫

At the Hop (Danny and the Juniors)

Blue Suede Shoes (Carl Perkins)

Bye, Bye Love (the Everly Brothers)

Diana (Paul Anka)

Honeycomb (Jimmy Rodgers)

Hound Dog (Elvis Presley)

I'm Moving On (Hank Snow)

Love Letters in the Sand (Pat Boone)

Love Me Tender (Elvis Presley)

Mary Lou (Ronnie Hawkins)

Rock Around the Clock (Bill Haley
        and the Comets)

Standing On the Corner (The Four Lads)

That'll Be the Day (Paul Anka)

Sh-boom (Crew Cuts)

Teen Angel (Mark Dinning)

The Purple People Eater (Sheb Wooley)

Whole Lot-ta Shakin' Goin' On
        (Jerry Lee Lewis)

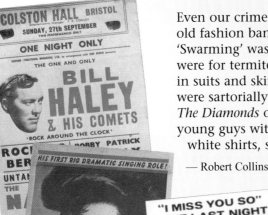

Even our crime was relatively benign. A good old fashion bank robbery was big news. 'Swarming' was for bees and 'home invasions' were for termites. We went to the office sedate in suits and skirts. Even our musical idols were sartorially correct: On fifties albums of *The Diamonds* or *The Four Lads* are clean-cut young guys with short haircuts, dark suits, white shirts, skinny neckties.

— Robert Collins, *Maclean's*, 3 April 1995

I'm so young and you're so old
This, my darling, I've been told
I don't care just what they say
'Cause forever I will pray

— "Diana," Paul Anka (1957)

▲ Fifteen year old **Paul Anka** was the "whiz kid from Ottawa who made it big on Tin Pan Alley." His hit single "Diana" topped the charts, selling over 3 million copies. It would go on to become one of the top ten best-selling North American singles of all time. He has written over 800 songs, many of which were hits for other singers. Among these were "My Way," "Put Your Head on My Shoulder," and "Having My Baby."

1950
—
1959

Brilliant Display

Glenn Gould Featured Symphony Concert
....

Glenn Gould, hunched on an ordinary chair over the keyboard of his grand piano, drew murmurs of comment from the first Sherbrooke Symphony Concert audience of the season…last night.

The brilliant 23-year-old Toronto-born pianist presented a fantastic figure. Unkempt, sandy hair tossing wildly, he jerked rhythmically with the music of the orchestra. His long, thin arms dangled limply at his sides, almost touching the stage floor. When he launched into the opening bars of Beethoven's Piano Concerto No. 4, he closed his eyes, tilted his head, and swayed low over the keys.

Those who weren't busy buzzing about his gestures heard one of the most masterfully-played piano concertos ever to be performed in Sherbrooke. Gould's technique and mechanical skill have already been hailed by critics throughout North America…

— Hugh Doherty, *Sherbrooke Daily Record*,
18 November 1955

▲ **Glenn Gould**, the famous Canadian pianist and composer, first played with the Toronto Symphony Orchestra at age 15 in 1947. He was eccentric, humming while he played, crouched over the piano and usually wearing a favourite cap. But he was "brilliant" and "complex," "his technique superb," said the critics when he gained international attention with Bach's *Goldberg Variations* in 1955.

(Canada's Sports Hall of Fame)

▲ **Vive "Le Rocket!"** Maurice "Rocket" Richard thrilled audiences throughout the 1940s and '50s, having 544 career goals and 82 goals during Stanley Cup play-offs. In 1955, he was suspended for the remainder of the season after he struck a Boston Bruins player with his stick and hit a linesman. Passionate Quebec fans rioted.

"I'm not a politician, I'm just a hockey player."

— Maurice Richard, 17 March 1955

"Every riot known to history has been the result of some im[bal]ance in our society or institution in which it has occurred. [The] fundamental moral imbalance behind this particular one [has] been evident for two and a half decades…"

"If you can't lick them in the alley, you can't lick them [in] the rink," has become a famous saying in English speak[ing] Canada… Unfortunately the adage had been taken literally [by] thousands of kids too ignorant to understand how untrue it [is. I] have seen plenty of plug-uglies who could have licked a sm[all] man like Howie Morenz in the alley, but I have yet to see [one] who could have licked him in the rink unless he used illegal [tac]tics…"

"Crude violence has been deliberately encouraged by so[me] business men who think it pays off at the box office, and by [one] or two coaches and managers whose teams are so crude th[ey] know they could not hope to win without it. Inevitably this [has] placed real hockey skill at a disadvantage, and it has cheat[ed,] frustrated and disgusted hundreds of thousands of us who ag[ain] and again have seen a first-class team disintegrated by alley t[ac]tics…"

— Hugh MacLennan, *Saturday Night*, 9 April 1955

(CP Photo)

▶ **"The Most Popular Man in Alberta"** Normie Kwong (on right), seen here with teammate Jackie Parker, led the Edmonton Eskimos to Grey Cup victories in 1954, '55, and '56.

◀ In September 1954, 16-year old **Marilyn Bell** became the first person to swim 52 km across Lake Ontario. She would also be the youngest ever to swim the English Channel and the Strait of Juan de Fuca. Writer June Callwood called her "a model hero — modest, intelligent, appreciative and charming."

"I thought my swim, if I finished it would be on the back pages of the papers. I thought I would just climb out and go home and a few of my friends would congratulate me… I didn't see the thousands of people at the waterfront… It was all like a dream or nightmare… The people in my boat…kept putting up signs that great sums of money would be given if I finished… It was an hour or two after I finished before I realized the sums were in thousands, not hundreds…"

— Marilyn Bell, September 1954

1956
Marlene Stewart wins 34
golf matches in a row

1956
Vancouver-born Yvonne De Carlo stars with
Charlton Heston in Hollywood blockbuster
The Ten Commandments

1957
Canada Council established to encourage
arts, humanities, and social sciences

"A Canadian is someone who drinks Brazilian coffee from an English teacup and munches French pastry, while sitting on his Danish furniture having just come home from an Italian movie in his German car. He picks up his Japanese pen and writes to his Member of Parliament to complain about the American take-over of the Canadian publishing business."

— Campbell Hughes, publishing executive, 1953

(ZUMA/Keystone Canada)

▶ **Jay Smith Silverheels**, from the Six Nations Reserve in Brantford, Ontario, had been a top boxer and lacrosse player. In Hollywood he made over 30 movies. He is best known for his role as "Tonto" in the popular *Lone Ranger* TV series and two movies produced in the 1950s.

(CBC Archives)

◀ **Juliette Cavazzi** was on network TV from 1954 to 1966. Hers was consistently one of CBC's most popular shows.

1950
—
1959

"In the present case the term [audience identification] is used to suggest that Juliette makes everybody feel that she might be their close personal friend — except women, who feel that Juliette might be them. Juliette, in short, is folks."

— "Why Should Juliette Knock Them Dead?" Barbara Moon in *Maclean's*, 26 April 1958

...Teenage spending in Canada has...reached $100 million a year according to a survey conducted among 150,000 high school students in Toronto, Montreal and Edmonton.... What kind of merchandise do teenagers buy with their own money? Clothes are the biggest single item... A quarter of all teenagers have a typewriter... Almost 80 per cent of them...own watches and the rest are going to get one as soon as they can. Almost 70 per cent have a bank account and most teenagers have a regular system of saving. Sixty per cent have cameras. They drink three bottles of pop a week, eat two candy bars (boys prefer Oh Henry; girls Sweet Marie), buy one record at about 90 cents for a 45-rpm disc and up to 98 cents for a 78.

— "The Scramble for the Teenage Dollar," John Clare, *Maclean's*, 14 September 1957

▲ **Elvis Presley,** clad in a gold lamé suit, "bumps and swivels" before a sold out crowd of 18 000 at Maple Leaf Gardens in 1957. When his first movie, *Love Me Tender*, opened in Toronto there was a mob scene as teens lined up before dawn. Parents despaired but teenage girls swooned over "Elvis the Pelvis."

27

1960
Paul Anka's
"Puppy Love" tops charts

1960
Yorkville, Toronto is
centre of Canada's
hippie movement

1962
University of Toro█
professors introdu█
electronic musi█

IN 1962, MOST OF THE POPULATION of Canada and the U.S. was school-aged and, for a few days, many of those youngsters thought that they were going to die in a nuclear war. U.S. President Kennedy imposed a blockade that pushed the Cuban Missile Crisis close to nuclear war before the Soviet Union backed down. That crisis may have been what led North American youth to create their own more liberated culture of peace and love.

Canadian author Marshall McLuhan redefined what culture meant in the new information age. Rather than just being swept along by cultural shifts, fads, and influences, people were thinking about how they were being changed by new technologies. The bulge in population known as the postwar baby boom had reached numbers which, combined with rising incomes, gave teenagers the power to shape the market for records, clothing, movies, cars, and magazines. Youth culture became the target of TV, film and record producers, advertisers, designers, manufacturers, and artists.

Youth-oriented, anti-establishment culture came to identify itself as "Pop Culture." Its images of rock bands, hippies, communes, anti-war and anti-nuclear protests, and race riots in the U.S. dominated the imagination of the era. However, for most, image did not match reality.

Most Canadians watched American TV shows, especially shows like *Ed Sullivan* which featured Canadian performers such as Wayne and Shuster and Robert Goulet. Also popular were Canadian-produced shows *Don Messer's Jubilee*, *Hockey Night in Canada*, and *Juliette*. Other forms of entertainment were bowling and American films.

In 1967, many more Canadians made their way to Expo '67 in Montreal than screamed through rock concerts, bought psychedelic clothing, attended Woodstock, smoked dope, dropped acid, or took part in protest marches. Nevertheless, the popular culture of passive "mere entertainment" was seen as the culture of the past, while the more activist, "meaningful" Pop Culture was declared to be the culture of the present and future.

Popular culture and "Pop Culture" came together in 1968 when Trudeaumania — the adoration of Prime Minister Pierre Trudeau, a charismatic figure of physical and intellectual vigour and a rebellious spirit — swept the country. The new culture was also seen in the adoption of much of the feminist agenda by both government and the media; in the popularity of cool poets and singer/songwriters like Leonard Cohen, Gordon Lightfoot, and Joni Mitchell; in questioning consumerism, nuclear weapons and war; and in the continuing national obsession with hockey.

fads

- Muscle cars: Mustang, Camaro, Corvette
- Windsurfing, skateboarding
- The Twist, the Jerk, the Watusi, the Mashed Potato
- Go-go dancing, transistor radios
- Electronic music in Moog Synthesizer
- Etch-a-Sketch, BB guns, Easy-Bake Ovens, Twister, Lava Lamps
- James Bond movies, toys and spy gadgets
- Afro, go-go boots, granny glasses, love beads, miniskirts

Peace.

◄ The first **Ookpik** was sewn out of sealskin by Jeannie Snowball, an Inuit from Fort Chimo, Quebec. The name means "happy little Arctic owl" and they became popular Canadian souvenirs.

(York University Archives)

"The car's future isn't rosy, it's not rosy at all... Already you can send almost anything anywhere by telegraph. Why have personal transportation when we have the videophone?"

— Marshall McLuhan, "The Future of the Car," *Maclean's*, September 1967

▶ **Barbie dolls,** in all the latest fashions, would become a huge, long-lasting seller.

◄ **Polaroid** introduced their first instant camera in 1948. However, it was expensive and used mainly by professionals. This $19.9█ Swinger Model came out in 1965, targeting a younger consumer.

(Courtesy W. McAskie)

1963

ordie Howe passes Rocket
chard's 545th Career Goal

1964

First Tim Horton's doughnut store
opens in Hamilton, Ontario

1965

Burton Cummings and others form rock band
Chad Allen and the Expressions
(The Guess Who)

*Nancy Green at the Winter
Olympics, Innsbruck, Austria, 1964.*

THE HIGH COST OF BEING A CANADIAN CHAMPION

With rare exceptions, it costs a talented youngster and his parents a small fortune to train for championships under Canadian do-it-yourself sports setup... Skier Nancy Green, 24 of Rossland B.C., won the World Cup last winter... To be a national ski-team member, she gave up university and raised $1,800 a year for travel. Since 1963, team education and training are subsidized at Notre Dame University, Nelson, B.C., and Nancy gets $5,000 from the B.C. government — AFTER her big win.

— Lynne Trimbee, *Chatelaine*, August 1967

(NAC Accession No. 1982-131-93)

EXPO GATES OPEN TO THE WORLD

*"Hey friend, say friend, come on over.
Looking for happiness. This is the place."*
(Theme chosen from 2200 entries from 35 countries)

This is a proud day for Montreal, for Quebec and above all for Canada.... No theme could have been more fitting for our time than "Man and his World."

— P.M. Pearson in his opening remarks, 27 April 1967

*Harry Jerome competing at the 1968 Olympic Games in Mexico.
Jerome set the 100m dash record at 10.0 seconds in 1960.*

(Courtesy F. Debusschere)

▲ **The miniskirt** — fashion versus practicality.

...Perhaps the blood lust of the spectator is a true reflection of the values of society. Is the exaggerated emotionalism of the spectator a safety value or a true representation of a socially immature population struggling to achieve self-realization in a technically sophisticated society?... What values are we transmitting to the next generation? Do our families, schools and communities demonstrate a different value system than that manifested in the arena?

— Dr. John Farina, *Weekend Magazine*, November 1969

> **"Violence is a quest for identity,
> the less identity the more violence."**

— Marshall McLuhan, 1964

"Dig Those Crazy Skurfers"

Skateboarding — or 'skurfing,' as it's also called — was started four years ago in California. Perhaps the surest sign of skateboarding's success is that it has already attracted detractors. The city council in Ottawa is considering a resolution to outlaw the sale of boards. And there's a spoilsport Toronto alderman who regularly issues statement of doom about 'the skateboard menace.'

— Jack Batten, *Maclean's*, 24 June 1965

(CBC Archives)

▲ "We had 4 million people looking at that show back in the '60s. No half hour musical show has ever attracted that since."

— Don Tremaine, emcee of *Don Messer's Jubilee* which aired from 1959 to 1969. Its cancellation sparked protests across the country and complaints during Question Period in the House of Commons.

(CBC Archives)

*Four strong winds that blow lone
Seven seas that run high
All these things that don't change*

◄ **Ian and Sylvia** Ian Tyson's "Fo Strong Winds," was recorded, not only by Ian and Sylvia, but by do of artists during the decade. Late would be revived by Canadian Ne Young.

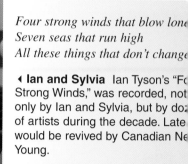

▶ **Gordon Lightfoot**

*If you could read my mind love,
What a tale my thoughts could tell...*

— Gordon Lightfoot, "If You Could Read My Mind," 1970

"The medium is the message."

— Marshall McLuhan, *Understanding Media*, 1964

...I find media analysis very much more exciting now simply because it affects so many more people. One measure of the importance of anything is: Who is affected by it? In our time, we have devised ways of making the most trivial event affect everybody. One of the consequences of electronic environments is the total involvement of people in people.

— Gerald Stearn's *Interview With Marshall McLuhan*, 1966

(CBC Archives)

▲ **Wayne and Shuster** Although seen here in a "hippie" sketch, Wayne and Shuster were noted for their take-offs on classical situations. Media guru Marshall McLuhan complimented them on their word games.

BEATLEMANIA
HITS TORONTO!

— 7 September 1964

The Beatles: A Wonder Drug

There they were — all four of the Beatles, live and in Toronto — and it was marvelous... I've never been so proud — of Toronto teens. They made a tremendous noise and shook the place with their foot-stomping; but they were the best behaved audience the Beatles had on their whole American tour. Two or three girls raced madly toward the stage at each of the two shows in a desperate attempt to be near their idols, but our efficient police (and they were everywhere you looked) moved in and carted off the weeping maidens before they made it.

— Michele Finney, *Toronto Daily Star*, 8 September 1964

Growing down: In most such matters of fad, teenagers are unwilling give a moment's heed to adult criticism — for they know that grown-ups eventually get wise. Growing down to teen tastes, adults took ove the twist, the Beatles, straight hair and tight pants, among dozens of other crazes. "Is nothing sacred any more?" moans one teenager.

— Cover story, *Time*, 29 January 1965

1967	1967	1968	1969
...ief Dan George delivers *Lament for ...federation*, a speech on the suffering of Aboriginal people in Canada	Feb: *Mr. Dressup* debuts on CBC television	Canadian Radio-television and Telecommunications Commission (CRTC) set up	Genevieve Bujold wins Best Actress Oscar for *Anne of the Thousand Days*

...rudeaumania! Canadians had never before seen anyone like Pierre Elliott ...deau in the House of Commons. People were mesmerized by him — he ...ught youthfulness and a promise of change. But Trudeau's appeal extended ...ond Parliament: he became a political pop star, attracting admirers whose ...dication rivalled that of Beatles fans.

"If all politicians were like Mr. Trudeau, there would be world peace."

— John Lennon, 1969

"He touched my hand; I'll never be able to wash it!"

— Teenage girl, 1968

MORALS: The Second Sexual Revolution

...The rebels of the '20s had Victorian parents who laid down a Victorian law; it was something concrete and fairly well defined to rise up against. The rebels of the '60s have parents with only the tattered remnants of a code... Adrift in a sea of permissiveness, [young people] have little to rebel against...

— Cover story, *Time*, 24 January 1964

John Lennon and Yoko Ono attend Peace Conference in Toronto

"We're here as a protest against violence... If we said anything in Canada, we knew that it would just go right away to the United States. We just knew that Canada would accept us..."

— John Lennon in an interview with Canadian rock reporter Ritchie Yorke, 1969

◄ **John Lennon** and Yoko Ono on a snowmobile on Ronny Hawkin's farm near Toronto, Ontario.

▼ **Woodstock** In the summer of 1969, 400 000 young people gathered on a farm near Woodstock, N.Y. for the biggest love-in of the decade. They sang in the rain and mud and listened to live music blasted from huge speakers.

(CP Photo)

I came upon a child of God; He was walking along the road And I asked him 'Where are you going?' This he told me: 'I'm going on down to Yasgur's Farm, gonna join in a rock & roll band I'm gonna camp out on the land and Try 'n get my soul free'...

— "Woodstock," Joni Mitchell, 1969

1960 — 1969

1970
First computer animation created by Nestor Burtnyk of Dauphin, Manitoba

1970
M.A.S.H. movie stars Canadian Donald Sutherland as Hawkeye

1970
The first IMAX developed by Canadians

SEVERAL EVENTS MARKED 1970 as a year of transition in popular culture from the peace-and-love hippie era of the 1960s to a decade shaped by anti-war and anti-establishment realism. Canada was traumatized by Quebec separatist bombings, the FLQ's kidnapping of British diplomat James Cross, and assassination of Quebec Labour Minister Pierre Laporte. Canadian university students blockaded border crossings to protest planned U.S. nuclear testing in the Arctic. At Kent State University in Ohio, soldiers shot and killed four students during an anti-Vietnam War protest. As trite as it seems by comparison, the event that most shocked the Pop Culture psyche was the break up of *The Beatles.*

The early 1970s were still dominated by the Pop Culture that had blossomed in the 1960s. Although young people were still dedicated to anti-establishment ideals, they were becoming voracious consumers of goods, design, and the arts. It was a time of social adjustment for the Pop Culture baby boomers who were now completing university, starting careers and families, or struggling to cope if they had "dropped out" of the traditional system and into alternative lifestyles.

The freedom tasted in the political, social, and sexual revolutions of the 1960s found new strength in an invigorated feminist movement that reached into all segments of society. Single parent families became more common as a result of changing attitudes to marriage and divorce. Population growth declined as many couples put off starting families or did not to have children at all. The idea that careers were to be lifelong and permanent was replaced by the understanding that jobs changed rapidly. Financial security was being eroded by inflation and, as the decade progressed, the pursuit of pleasure became the goal of many.

Disco, which Hollywood captured in *Saturday Night Fever*, replaced rock as the musical rage and lifestyle choice. The American withdrawal from Vietnam ended the era of the anti-war demonstration, but anti-war sentiment was kept alive in movies like *Apocalypse Now*, and in the hit film and television comedy, *M.A.S.H.*

Clothing design shifted to the flashy, glitzy designs of the disco era. Anything with the designation "herbal" or "organic" was a hit. Meanwhile, the promise of computer-based mass entertainment and communication media was becoming more plausible. Videotape players and video cameras became household items, opening new movie rental markets while eroding the influence of the established TV networks. Rap emerged as a new music phenomenon, while the clothing and attitudes of its black urban origins became the new bad-boy style to be imitated.

fads

- Dreadlocks, the wedge, shag hairdos
- Hot pants, bell bottoms, Roots, T-shirts with sayings
- Punk music/style, mood rings, charm bracelets
- Pet rocks, happy faces, valley girl talk, streaking
- Customized vans, bumper stickers
- Saturday Night Live, SCTV, The Brady Bunch, Sesame Street, Happy
- GI Joe, Transformers, Star Wars, E.T., Nintendo, Pac Man, Game Boy, Teenage Mutant Ninja Turtles, Dungeons and Dragons

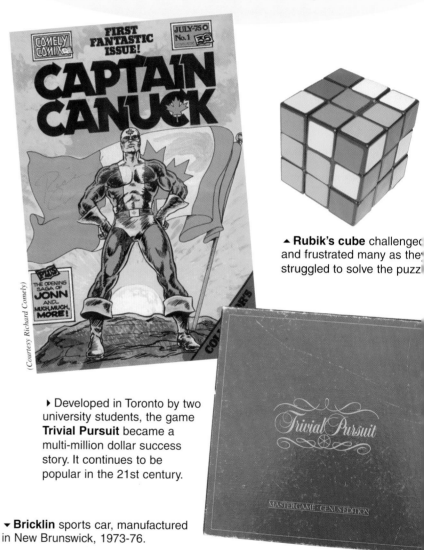

(Courtesy Richard Comely)

▲ **Rubik's cube** challenged and frustrated many as they struggled to solve the puzzle

▸ Developed in Toronto by two university students, the game **Trivial Pursuit** became a multi-million dollar success story. It continues to be popular in the 21st century.

▾ **Bricklin** sports car, manufactured in New Brunswick, 1973-76.

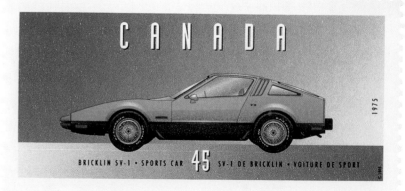

(Canada Post Corporation 1975, Reproduced with Permission)

"…Here's a shot. Henderson makes a wild stab for it and falls… Here's another shot. Right in front. They score! Henderson scores for Canada!"

— Foster Hewitt, Moscow's Palace of Sport, 28 September 1972

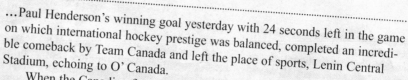

…Paul Henderson's winning goal yesterday with 24 seconds left in the game on which international hockey prestige was balanced, completed an incredible comeback by Team Canada and left the place of sports, Lenin Central Stadium, echoing to O' Canada.

When the Canadian fans, more than 2,500 of them finished with the anthem, they started to chant "We're Number 1." The final score was 6-5 for the Canadians and a series victory of four wins, three losses and a tie.

Inside the Team Canada dressing room, there was a feeling of frantic pride. Not a lot of noise, no victory champagne, just a team of proud men making assertive statements.

"It was the biggest thrill of my career to be named to this team," said Henderson, the left-winger who has skated for four years with Toronto Maple Leafs to modest reviews. "The next biggest thrill was to make the team.

"And now, three winning goals in a row. Who can believe it?"

— "From Russia with Glory," Dan Proudfoot, *Globe and Mail*, 29 September 1972

(Montreal Gazette/NAC PA 209772)

Canada's first Hall of Fame member, Fergie Jenkins used pinpoint control and effectively changed speeds to win 284 games… A diligent workhorse, Jenkins used an easy, uncomplicated motion to reach the 20 win mark seven times and capture the National League Cy Young Award in 1974.

— Baseball Hall of Fame

1970
—
1979

…uebec speed skater **Gaetan Boucher**, seen …e training at the 1976 Innusbruck Olympics, … hailed as a national hero after he won two … medals and a bronze at Sarajevo in 1984.

▲ **Ferguson Jenkins**, pitcher for the Chicago Cubs, in action against the Montreal Expos, 19 September 1970, Montreal, Quebec.

We view content we dislike, content that is frivolous, unsatisfying, unrewarding… People love TV. They love the ease of viewing and the ease of distribution: Video pictures delivered right to the home. Somebody's going to figure out how to give this medium more satisfying content as we head toward a completely visual culture.

— Paul Klein, TV Guide, 1971

Since the issues are getting "hot," it would be a huge advantage to shift the main broadcast coverage to radio. Radio is a "hot" medium and is indispensable when the issues get hot. TV is a fantasy medium, and has good reason to be called "cool."

— Marshall McLuhan's advice to Prime Minister Trudeau during the 1979 election campaign

(Canada Post Corporation 1979. Reproduced with Permission)

▲ **Quebec Carnival** stamp.

1973
The Royal Canadian Air Farce debuts on radio

1973
First microcomputer appears

1974
Mordecai Richler's *The Apprenticeship of Duddy Kravitz* stars Canadian Micheline Lanctot

1974
NFB computer animation f Hunger/La Faim first in the w to use character animatio

Should the following be sold or shown without restriction?

	Eng. % Yes	Fr. % Yes
War Toys	35	13
War Movies	47	25
War Stories on TV	51	29

— *Maclean's,* Goldfarb Report on Canadian Culture and Violence, 1970

(*CBC Archives*)

▲ **The Friendly Giant** Generations of Canadian children enjoyed and learned from Bob Homme, the Friendly Giant, and the puppet characters Rusty and Jerome through song, conversation, and gentle story.

◄ **Sesame Street's** Big Bird with guest star Canadian singer Buffy Sainte-Marie. The show transformed educational TV for children and spun off into toys, feature films, magazines, public service commercials, fashion design, records, and cartoons.

▲ Montrealer **William Shatner** (left) with Kelley DeForrest and Leonard Nimoy in *Star Trek*, 1968. Shatner was the hero of the Starship Enterprise's bridge through the early years of the series, and his crisp, choppy style of speaking became the object of man comedians' routines. *Star Trek* began in the '60s, reached its heig of popularity in the '70s, and continued into the 21st century.

"My first recollection of acting was in a summer camp that my au ran in the Laurentians up near Ste Agathe. I can recall a parent visiting day, a Sunday, when we put on a skit. It must have bee during the War because it had something to do with the War. T subject must have touched the people watching because I ca remember people crying, the parents crying. It was my first sens of the kind of thing that can be effective on the stage."

— William Shatner, *Oh, I had dreams*

Sesame Street was go-go-go, high energy, a busy atmosphere. *Mr. Dressup* and *The Friendly Giant* were for "quiet time." They were welcoming, peaceful, nurturing. The children felt part of the show. Overall they presented a calming, caring environment.

— Barbara Van Mol, babysitter

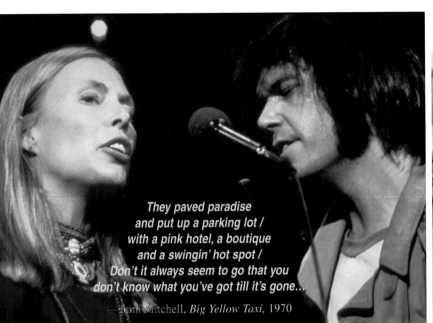

*They paved paradise
and put up a parking lot /
with a pink hotel, a boutique
and a swingin' hot spot /
Don't it always seem to go that you
don't know what you've got till it's gone...*

— Joni Mitchell, *Big Yellow Taxi*, 1970

The Last Waltz starring **Joni Mitchell** and **Neil Young**, 1978. Canadian singers Joni Mitchell and Neil Young became international stars with a very solid home ience, an audience helped along by Canadian Content Regulations that made it that 35% of the music on radio had to have been developed in this country.

▲ A combination of situation comedy and soap opera, **King of Kensington** featuring Al Waxman was a favourite with Canadian audiences for years. Set in a working-class neighbourhood and peopled by easy-going and mildly eccentric folk it contrasted the highly polished and high-paced American comedies.

*said a hip hop the hippie to the hippie
e hip hip hop, a you don't stop
e rock it to the bang bang boogie say up jumped the boogie
the rhythm of the boogie the beat...*

Sugar Hill Gang, "Rapper's Delight," first rap recording, 1979

tially, **rap** was a way for the black and Latino urban communities to express emselves artistically. It originated from West Africa where "men of words" re held in high regard. Over 100 years later, rap became a street art.

(CBC Archives)

Born and raised in Montreal, **Oscar Peterson** is one of the st admired jazz musicians and composers in the world.

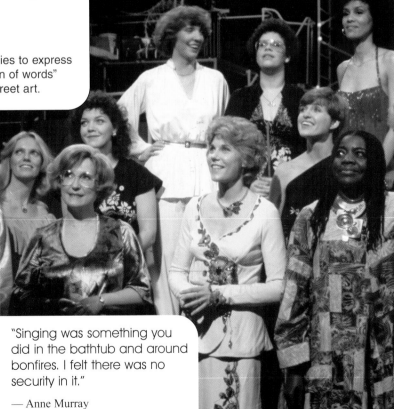

"Singing was something you did in the bathtub and around bonfires. I felt there was no security in it."

— Anne Murray

(CBC Archives)

▲ **Anne Murray**, a Physical Education teacher from Springhill, Nova Scotia, became the laid-back darling of the pop music scene in the 1970s and '80s. Her enormous success here and abroad was unprecedented for a Canadian. She was a featured performer for several American presidents.

1980 - 1989

1980
Terry Fox's
Marathon of Hope

1981
The Inuit Broadcasting
Corporation (IBC) established

FOR A FEW MONTHS in the mid-'80s, the media were riveted by the exploits of two American TV evangelists, Jim and Tammy Baker, their slick, seedy excesses, and subsequent disgrace and jailing. Meanwhile, Canadians were stunned when sprinter Ben Johnson was stripped of his Olympic gold medal because of the use of illegal drugs. These icons of popular culture were better known in disgrace than in success. They were symbols for a decade which had begun in excess and then was humbled by its excesses.

By the 1980s, the once revered Pop Culture movement had disappeared and melded with popular culture. The term "Pop" had come to mean tasteless, over-produced, and predictable. It was seen as no more than the self-serving output of greedy producers of music, film, videos, magazines, and advertising. As always, mass culture would have to re-invent itself to be cool, new, and bold again.

Changes in technology shaped popular culture in the 1980s. CD recordings replaced audio cassette tapes, and VCRs were found in most homes. People waited for films to be released on video rather than going to theatres — unless, of course, the movie had dazzling visual and sound effects.

The "disco-glitter" movement gave way to the fitness and dancewear look inspired, in part, by break-dancing, jogging, and *Flashdance*. By the mid-1980s, anti-establishment punk, grunge, and rap music, and subsequently their related styles of clothing, design, and graphics, had replaced more conventional rock and disco. By the end of the decade the styles suggested by these rawer music movements had found their way into the mainstream popular culture in the tattered, worn, and ripped clothing styles of the grunge movement, in deliberately "unsophisticated" looking graphics, videos and advertising, and in "retro" tastes.

There was a rapid expansion of computer ownership and use, as well as hand-held video games, but also a surprising swing back to low-tech games like the Canadian board game, *Trivial Pursuit*. Kids of all ages rediscovered action comic books. *Green Hornet, Batman,* and *Superman* became desirable collector items. Sports collectibles, especially hockey and baseball cards, became the rage. In films, the violent exploits of super popular, high-tech heroes such as Rambo, Rocky, and Mad Max seemed to suggest that nobility and justice could be achieved by simple-minded and supernaturally lucky lone warriors.

Cable television was introduced and Canadian produced television shows such as The *Degrassi* Series, *Road to Avonlea,* and *Beachcombers* led the industry in exporting Canadian content to over 80 countries.

fads

- Fluorescent colours
- Jelly shoes, mohawk hairdos
- Bungee jumping, breakdancing
- Prime-time soaps, mini-series
- Minivans, SUVs
- Swatch watches, shoulder pads
- Lean meals, 'diet' shakes
- Atari home video games
- Extra-large "phat" blue jeans and shorts
- Jackets with sports logos, 'Roots' look

"You couldn't play with the other little girls if you didn't have one."

— Patricia LeRoux, who asked her newlywed uncle and his bride to sleep with her doll when she left it at their wedding reception. They did.

▸ Parents lined up overnight in snowstorms and had shoving matches in toy stores to get their kids a **Cabbage Patch Kid.** The dolls, which came with their own name and birth certificate, were a "must have."

VCRs: Coming on Strong
Santa's hottest gift is a magic box that revolutionizes viewing

— *Time,* 24 December 1984

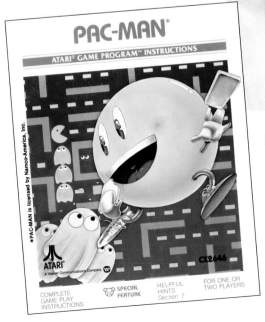

PAC-MAN*

ATARI® GAME PROGRAM™ INSTRUCTIONS

*PAC-MAN is licensed by Namco-America, Inc.

ATARI
A Warner Communications Company

CX2646

COMPLETE GAME PLAY INSTRUCTIONS   SPECIAL FEATURE   HELPFUL HINTS Section 7   FOR ONE OR TWO PLAYERS

▲ The **home office** was gain in popularity as personal computers became available.

◂ Home **video games** like Pac-Man were revolutionary. Hand-held games like these were not just fads — some thought they were dangerou obsessions.

The Mall "Garden of Eden in a Box"

The mall is [a]...year-round carnival, the cathedral of the postwar culture, the Garden of Eden in a box...a utopia fashioned by the not-so-quite-invisible hand of merchandising.... This is the culmination of the postwar Highway Comfort Culture which has matched the aspirations, obsessions, social mores, and upward mobility of the middle class... Its space is special because it is protected. The mall banishes outside threats of disruption and distraction.... The mall is also controlled space...a magic theatre... The mall is a visual experience. It is TV that you walk around in. "People watching" is what people do in the mall when they aren't "looking for something" to buy.

— William Severini Kowinski, *The Malling of America, An Inside Look at the Great Consumer Paradise*, 1985

.ONING THE CONSUMER CULTURE: *How ternational Marketing Sells the Western Lifestyle*

.e common theme of transatlantic culture is con-
.mption... Advertisers rely on a few repetitive themes:
.ppiness, youth, success, status, luxury, fashion and
.auty. Social contradictions and class differences are
.asked and workplace conflicts are not shown...
.obal marketing strategy is so effective that conscious
.bversion is hardly needed. The message "we will sell
.u a culture," has resulted in the global advertising
.mpaign,.... Increasingly, advertising campaigns are
.ned at the vast numbers of poor in Third World
.untries... Advertising of skin-lightening products
.rsuades the African women to be ashamed of their
.vn color and try to be white.

Noreene James, *Cultural Survival Quarterly*, 1983

.e are being swallowed up by the popular culture of
.e United States, but then the Americans are being
.allowed up by it too. It's just as much a threat to
.nerican culture as it is to ours... The Canadian iden-
.y is bound up with the feeling that the end of the
.inbow never falls on Canada.

Northrop Frye on Canadian Identity, 15 April 1982

(CP Photo/Dave Buston)

▲ **West Edmonton Mall**, the largest in the world, featuring over 800 stores, a hotel, a water park, and a skating rink. It catered to consumers who believed in the "shop until you drop" philosophy of the 1980s.

1983	1983	1984
Timothy Findley's *The Wars* made into movie	Canadian documentary *If You Love This Planet* labelled "political propaganda" by U.S. government yet wins Academy Award	Cirque du Soleil formed

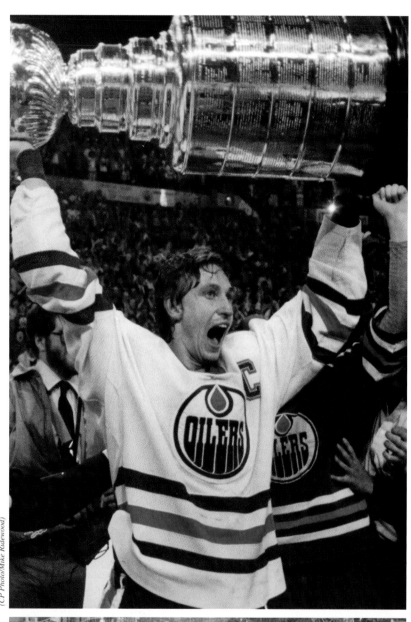

(CP Photo/Mike Ridewood)

"THE GREAT ONE!"

"You spend years and years of work and you finally win the Stanley Cup. There is nothing like it."

— Wayne Gretzky after Edmonton wins the Stanley Cup in 198[

"Canadians are very proud of their country. I know I am.... One thing we have is the game of hockey. That's ours. And I always try to remember that."

— Wayne Gretzky

◀ **Wayne Gretzky** holds up the 1984 Stanley Cup for fans.

Celebrities are invariably accepted as instant authorities.... Synthetic celebrities are, after all, but reflections of ourselves...

— Barbara Goldsmith, *The New York Times*, 1986

(CP Photo)

▲ **World Cup Victory** Tens of thousands of Italian Canadians spilled onto the streets of big cities like Toronto in a frenzy of celebration in 1988.

▲ Skater Brian Orser carries the Canadian flag at the opening ceremonies of the **Calgary Olympics** in February 1988.

1984

Bryan Adams sweeps Juno Awards with Best Album,
Best Composer, Male Vocalist, Producer, and Writer

1985

21 Mar: Wheelchair athlete Rick Hansen
begins Man in Motion world tour

the *degrassi* series

▲ TV's *Degrassi* series engaged teens with depictions of the struggles teens face growing up in modern urban settings. Siluck Saysanasy is seen on right.

I was 12 years old when I landed the part of Yick Yu in *Degrassi Junior High*. The thinking behind hiring kids without any previous acting experience was to get raw and believable portrayals of the characters that they played. In the beginning we had some great press and some really horrible press. I don't think that any of us ever thought that the show would become the phenomenon that it became. The producers would take our real life experiences and incorporate into them onto the scripts. We, as young actors, also had an unbelievable amount of input in regards to the story lines. We would read through the scripts and the producers and writers would sit there with pens at the ready and listen to us while we chopped up the script. We would say "Kids would never say this!!!" or "Are you kidding? Do you really think kids are that stupid?!!" I think one of the main reasons that the show was so successful was because the producers had the courage to listen to us and actually produce a show that portrayed what we had shared with them about our real life experiences. After all, we were the same age as their target audience. And *Degrassi*, to this day after seventeen years, is still aired around the world.

— Siluck Saysanasy, actor and assistant director, Toronto, 2003

Great White North When *SCTV* performers Rick Moranis and Dave Thomas were told to create a sketch that was totally Canadian, they decided that going overboard with stereotypes was the only way to mock the regulation. Instead it created a mania for anything to do with "belching hosers" Bob and Doug Mackenzie. Take off, eh?

> Eating, drinking, or talking about food occur nine times an hour in peak time [on TV].
>
> — *Globe and Mail*, 14 May 1985

Louis del Grande was the bespectacled, balding, and muddled hero in **Seeing Things**, a mix of science fiction, comedy, and detective elements. The show was a hit with Canadians for several seasons. Guest stars Canadian prima ballerina Karen Kain and her actor/producer husband Ross Petty are shown with del Grande below.

(SCTV)

ETHICS IN BROADCASTING:

- A ban on abusive or discriminatory material based on race, ethnicity, colour, religion, age, sex, sexual orientation, marital status, or physical or mental handicap.

- The encouragement of positive social behaviour and attitudes in children's programs.

- Fair treatment of all sides of controversial public issues.

- Adequate opportunities for presenting religious messages that do not attack other races or religions.

- A commitment on the part of station management not to editorialize in news programming, or select items based on personal preferences or prejudices.

(Canadian Broadcast Standards Council (CBSC), 1988)

▶ **Filmmakers Extraordinaire** David Cronenberg (left) and Norman Jewison are in good company with fellow Canadians and international award winners such as Claude Jutra *(Mon Oncle Antoine)*, Denys Arcand *(Jesus of Montreal),* and Atom Egoyan *(The Sweet Hereafter).*

"No one was really interested in Canadian talent.... I realized that even well-established TV talents like Wayne and Shuster were not treated with respect until they appeared on the *Ed Sullivan Show* from New York.... Why did we take such pride in the Robertson screwdriver and ignore a Christopher Plummer? Just think — the Tony Award-winning actress, Amanda Plummer, would have been Canadian had her father been appreciated at home."

— "The Power of Film and Its Influence," address by Norman Jewison, 5 April 1984

◀ Canada's **Michael J. Fox** starred in the blockbuster, "cross-generational film" *Back to the Future* and its two sequels whi also playing Alex Keaton on the popular TV series, *Family Ties*. Fox described the film a "comedy-action-fantasy-adventure-comin of age film." He is pictured here with co-sta Christopher Lloyd.

(Universal Pic/ZUMA Press/KEYSTONE Press. © Copyright 1985 by Courtesy of Universal Pic)

Mega-Musicals

Even while I was still a teenager at theatre school in 1985 I got caught up in the exploding world of the big, highly developed musicals that came to be known as mega-musicals. Broadway had always been the hub of the world for doing these huge, expensive, big audience shows but starting with *Cats* and then going on to shows like *Phantom of the Opera, Les Miserables, Sunset Boulevard,* and so on. There was a phenomenon of duplicate musical theatre shows being put on for multi-year runs in cities like Toronto, Vancouver, and Calgary. Under a Canadian company called Livent we started to originate musicals in this country and export them internationally. There were thousands of people in Canada involved in performance, marketing, and development of mega-musicals like *Ragtime* and *Fosse* and millions of people attended the shows. Eventually the overexpansion of the form led to people getting tired of the style of entertainment and probably the cost of tickets added to the eventual move back to Broadway of the big musicals. Some of us ended up following the work to New York. The time of the megamusical was a really exciting era because for the first time in decades people seemed to fall in love with getting all dressed up to go out to a big evening at live theatre.

— Guy Kwan, managing producer, Broadway, NYC

1988

Actress Jill Hennessy makes film debut in
Dead Ringers with her real life twin sister Jacqui

1989

Canadian novel *Shoeless Joe* made into
Hollywood movie, *Field of Dreams*

Bryan Adams was a sensation of the '80s. His boyish
... look, rock sound, and slightly distant persona made
... successes on rock videos, live performances, and TV
... mercials seem almost inevitable.

▸ **The School Dance** Change and continuity.

CRTC approves licence for Much Music station
— 2 April 1984

"[Television is]…the single
most important development
in communication since the
invention of the written language."

— Moses Znaimer

(Brian Willer)

▴ Exercise was a new trend
in the '80s and no activity was
more popular than **aerobics.**

twirling, whirling dance revolution

breakdancing.

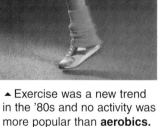

…[B]lack and Hispanic youths…developed
[breakdancing]…as a diversion during
truces in endless rounds of gang warfare
and streetfighting… The activity remained
in the U.S. ghettos until last year's hit film
Flashdance. And in the past year white and
black Canadian teenagers have started to
breakdance in everything from impromptu
amateur street acts to staged
professional performances
in nightclubs from Halifax
to Vancouver.

— *Maclean's*, 19 March 1984

Whatever they're doing on
television… they're going to
be doing on the street.

— *Channels*, 1987

BY THE LAST DECADE of the millennium, the baby boomers had reached middle age. Most of their parents were still alive and had become grandparents or even great-grandparents. Canadians had not faced a major war in half a century and had enjoyed the longest stretch of economic prosperity in history. "Popular culture" and "culture" had become virtually identical. New art forms, modes of expression, and methods of communication which had not even been dreamed of at the start of the century were now commonplace.

Despite a recession at the beginning of the decade, the 1990s was marked by the dizzying consumption of electronic goods, imported luxury cars, passenger vans and SUVs, and expensive vacations. The look of older urban and suburban areas was being altered by the construction of ostentatious monster homes. Home access to almost all of the world's knowledge and entertainment was now available to growing numbers of Canadians via the Internet. Satellite dishes delivered 300 television channels to households that 40 years before had had access to only one or two. By the late 1990s, TV was catering to the wealthy older generation with a profusion of news, sports, stock market, lifestyle, and shopping channels. Music video, cartoon, comedy, and x-treme sports channels entertained the growing youth market.

The children and grandchildren of the baby boomers had more disposable income than any generation in history. This "mall generation" made shopping a major leisure activity. Popular magazines, video games, blockbuster films, ever more powerful computers, cell phones, CDs and mini-discs, and name brand designer clothes became expressions of status and popular culture. The relative wealth and rebelliousness of youth gave popular culture its energy — from skateboarding, snowboarding, and x-treme sports to graffiti tagging, gangsta rap music and clothing, and the rise of youth gangs.

Traditional culture flourished as well. There was a substantial growth in the number of, and international praise for, Canadian books, magazines, films, and TV shows. Attendance at both small and large theatre performances, opera, ballet, art galleries, rodeos, fall fairs, and music and book festivals grew throughout the decade.

Multiculturalism began to flourish as various ethnic influences became part of the cultural mainstream. Ethnic foods, world music, and multicultural television were some of the most obvious signs of this cultural change. Most Canadian nominees and winners of major Canadian and international book prizes were not born in Canada, a fact that was hardly noticed by the end of the century.

fads

- Baseball caps worn backwards
- Revival of swing dancing
- The Simpsons, Jurassic Park, Titanic, Mr. Bean
- Goosebumps books by R.L. Stine
- Virtual reality computer games
- Snowboarding, skateboarding
- Body piercing, tattoos
- Grunge look

SUPER STAR
HOCKEY 92

▲ **Sports cards**, once reserved for professional athletes, have become gimmick to celebrate young amateu

◀ **Basketball** fans wear their favourite team's logo.

THE CULT YOU'RE IN: What does it mean when a whole culture dreams the same dream?

A long time ago, without even realizing it, you were recruited into a cult…a cult member showed up and made a beautiful presentation…she was offering something to give your life meaning. She was wearing Nikes and a Planet Hollywood cap.

— *Adbusters*, Summer 1998

Trial Begins in Dungeons & Dragons' Killing: Brother, Two Friends Charged With Murdering California Girl

Obsession with Role Playing Games?

Prosecutors claimed that the killing of 12 year-old Stephanie Crowe in 1998 was spurred by an obsession with role playing games such as Dungeons & Dragons.

— 12 January 1999, APBnews.com

RULES FOR CHILDREN'S PROGRAMMING

- In live action programming, only violence essential to the plot or character development may be depicted.
- In animation programming, violence cannot be the central theme.
- No programming shall contain realistic scenes of violence which minimize or gloss over the consequences of violent acts.
- No programming shall invite imitation of dangerous acts seen on the screen.

— *Canadian Broadcasting Standards Council*

▲ The movies, the modern shopping mall, native Canadian dance and culture all come together in this moment at the mall in Prince Rupert, British Columbia. Photographer William deKay brilliantly captured the essence of popular **rural culture** in his book *Down Home.*

◄ **Silken Laumann** refused to let a major laceration stop her from competing at the 1996 Olympics. She won a silver medal and became an inspiration not only as a sportswoman, but also as a sports hero.

(CP Photo/Hans Deryk)

Canada's **Donovan Bailey** wins the men's 0m event at the 1996 Olympics in Atlanta.

Silken's cold costs a Gold
But positive test not likely to keep her out of Olympics

…Pan-Am Games officials in Argentina decided yesterday to strip Laumann and her quadruple teammates of their gold medals in light of Laumann's positive drug test for the banned substance pseudophedrine, a synthetic match to the stimulant ephedrine… Laumann said she declared to testing officials she was taking Benadryl after each of her races on the weekend. "(When) I said Benadryl, I didn't raise any questions and I didn't raise any eyebrows," said the visibly angered Laumann. "No one asked, 'How much Benadryl are you taking? What kind of Benadryl are you taking?'"… Ironically, because she did not test positive after her victory in Saturday's single sculls, she gets to keep her gold medal for that race…

— Steve Buffery, *Toronto Sun*, 24 March 1995

1990
—
1999

43

1994

Lacrosse designated Canada's National Summer Sport; hockey is Canada's National Winter Sport

1994

Mainframe Entertainment of Vancouver *Reboot* series is first computer animated TV series

1994

John Part (a.k.a. Darth Maple) of Osha Ontario wins World Darts Championsh

...Smile!

When you think about what inventions have completely altered society, a couple of biggies top the list. There's fire, the wheel, the fridge, and so on.

But in recent time, the one invention that really sticks out is obvious. The easy-to-use, two-pound, hand-held home video camera. Before videos, we had to be content just to hear about how cute our nephews were at their grade three French immersion Christmas concert. Now we get to watch all two and a half hours. And they say vacation slide shows were bad.

But before video, if you were asked, "Who ya gonna believe, the low-down, lying, good-for-nothing nobody or the one who has taken an oath to serve and protect?" You wouldn't be blamed for pickin' up the latter.... But now it turns out that every time there's a video camera around, the low-down, lying, good-for-nothing nobodies are being wacked with sticks on the L.A. freeway, rode around like donkeys by a bunch of Airborne.

But it you ever find yourself on the wrong end of a nightstick, you'll thank your lucky stars someone, somewhere has you perfectly framed with that easy-to-use, dummy-proof, auto-focus and zoom.

— SMILE! First aired as a 'Streeters: rant and rave' by Rick Mercer on *This Hour Has 22 Minutes*, 27 February 1995

▲ **Jim Carrey** in *Ace Ventura: Pet Detective*

"What matters is that he attained a position of public recogni tion higher than that of any other Canadian movie star since Mary Pickford, and that it all began with a distinctly Canadi if not Southern Ontarian, tradition: with a kid sitting at hom watching way too much TV beamed in from someplace else

— Geoff Pevere and Greig Dymond in *Mondo Canuck*, 1996

▲ On stage in *Phantom of the Opera*, on television in *Party of Five*, and on film in the *Scream* movies, Canadian **Neve Campbell** seemed to be everywhere in the late '80s and '90s.

THE JOKE'S ON THEM

Hey, Royal Canadian Air Farce! You're the number one Canadian show on the CBC. On good nights, you outdr *Hockey Night In Canada*. You deserve something special.

— Jim Slotek, *Toronto Sun*, 3 April 1996 when the CBC proposed a 5% cut for the *Royal Canadian Air Farce*

"Political satire is supposed to be politically incorrect that's the point! I think it's a nuisance that provokes u into being more thoughtful and inventive.... It nudge everyone to a different level of comedy. Even if a jo is politically incorrect, if a joke is really funny, the aud ence won't filter the laughs. They may feel guilty abo it later, but they'll laugh."

— Roger Abbot who stars with Luba Goy, Don Ferguson, and John Morgan in the *Royal Canadian Air Farce*

"... I came into this [Canadian] culture as a child who didn't speak English, and came at a point when this other personality wasn't wholly formed, and suddenly I had to absorb another culture and I remember being aware of that. I remember the things I had to do in order to be like the other kids. That does have an effect on you and you realize that personality is something that you construct."

— Atom Egoyan, writer/director in *MovieMaker* magazine

The **Vancouver Dragon Dance** is but one of the many festivals and activities celebrating Canada's ethnic diversity. Others include Toronto's Caribana (featured on this book's cover), and Caravan celebrations in several cities and community parties across the country.

▾ Quebec's **Cirque du Soleil** changed the notion of what the circus was and fascinated the world. Originally using disenfranchised youths to perform in their artistically and physically stunning performances, *Cirque* reminded audiences that art and popular entertainment can be one and the same.

(CP Photo/Journal de Montreal-Luc Belisle)

FOREIGN CONTENT IN THE CANADIAN CULTURAL MARKET:

70% of the music on Canadian radio stations
60% of all English-language television programming available in Canada
33% of all French-language television programming available in Canada
70% of Canadian book market
83% of the Canadian newstand market for magazines
84% of retail sales of sound recordings in Canada (including 69% of French-language retail sales)
95% of the feature films screened in Canadian theatres (this % is higher in English-language markets)
86% of prime-time English-language dramas on Canadian television
75% of prime-time drama on Canadian French-language television

— Statistics from a speech by Victor Rabinovitch (then Assistant Deputy Minister for Cultural Development and Heritage) in "The Cultural and Free Trade Quandry."

▸ Parents and others protest against commercial television in schools.

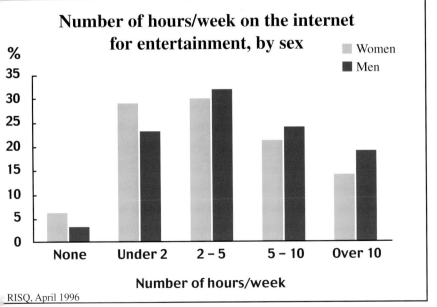

Number of hours/week on the internet for entertainment, by sex

■ Women
■ Men

%
35
30
25
20
15
10
5
0

None   Under 2   2 – 5   5 – 10   Over 10

Number of hours/week

How Seventeen *Undermines Young Women*

…An average issue of *Seventeen* contains about eight to 12 fashion and beauty features, taking up two-thirds of the magazine's editorial content. There is usually one story about a new exercise or fitness regime, one story in which the "average" looking girl gets a makeover, numerous pages of makeup tricks and techniques, mini stories on what's new in the fashion world… For a magazine aimed at teenage girls, *Seventeen* does a lot of reporting to men. In 1991, 61 of the celebrities profiled…were men while only 20 were women… One in only two articles in 1992 about eating disorders among teenage girls was written by a man... The whole July 1992 issue was devoted to "One Hundred Guys We Love."….

— Kimberly Phillips, *Extra,* Jan/Feb 1993 (*Seventeen* is the most widely read magazine among teenage girls in North America)

1990
–
1999

TALES OF A CANADIAN ANIMATOR

In 1995 I went to work for "Chuck Jones Film Productions" in Los Angeles, California whose agenda was to create new animated shorts starring the classic "Looney Tunes" characters for Warner Brothers. These shorts were to be shown in movie theatres before feature films like they were originally intended.

Having grown up in Oakville, Ontario, it was pretty exciting and more than a bit scary to end up working with these people who were legends thirty years before I was born! One memorable afternoon was spent with Chuck Jones while just the two of us watched his old cartoons and he told me stories of the crazy old days in Hollywood. What made it more manageable was the number of people in the animation industry who had come out of Canada and who were working in L.A. at the time. Canada had always had a great reputation for producing animated films, especially from the National Film Board and Sheridan College, so that made the job of trying to fit in a bit easier. The Jones studio was where I had the most fun working. It was a small crew with a lot of Canadians from Sheridan's animation program. In 1997, Warner Brothers pulled the plug and our little group of Canadians moved over to DreamWorks and we were absorbed into their giant movie making machine.

Fortunately change is happening rapidly and digital technology is really exploding the way people view animation. The nineties were a time of re-thinking and re-inventing and for the public and the movie industry, re-discovering, what animation could be. It's going to be interesting to see what form animation studios are going to take in the next few years.

— Cory Wilson, animator, Los Angeles, California

Too Few Animated Women Break the Disney Mold

What messages do the immensely popular Disney animations convey about women?... [There] are a series of stock female characters:...the [increasingly] curvaceous, slightly fretful, but essentially innocuous heroine (*Little Mermaid, Pocahontas*); the touchingly strong contemporary heroine, determined to fulfill her own destiny without ruining her hair (Belle in *Beauty and the Beast*); and the larger than-than-life matron who is either menacing (Cruella de Vil in *101 Dalmatians)*, or comic (the Queen of Hearts in *Alice in Wonderland*), or both (the Ugly stepsisters in *Cinderella*).... There aren't many heroines that are successful and unattractive, either; in animation or in live action movies. The modern cartoon heroine may aspire to a career; but if she doesn't snag a handsome prince, too, she hasn't really succeeded....

— Susan Riley, *Ottawa Citizen,* 1988

▲ It caused national outrage when the **Disney** Corporation bought the copyright to the image of the Canadian Mounties. Some though the Americans had symbolically stolen our national identity. In true Canadian fashion a compromise was reached. The Mounties are still Canadian.

▲ **Jean Chrétien** on trombone and **Dan Aykroyd** on harmonica.

One rumour had it that Canadian actor Dan Aykroyd was in town to audition local talent for another "blues brother." This version of "Le the Good Times Roll" may have stopped the search. The truth is the Ottawa native stopped off at the Governor General's residence to pi up an Order of Canada before heading over to 24 Sussex.

— Mark S. Bell, *Privileged Access,* 2000

1999

Joni Mitchell inducted into the Grammy Hall of Fame for *Blue* album (1971)

1999

30 Dec: Eaton's officially becomes part of Sears Canada

1999

Wayne Gretzky and Nancy Greene are named athletes of the century

▶ **Celine Dion** hosting the 20th ADISQ gala in Montreal, November 1998. A classic "small town girl makes good," Dion, along with manager/husband René, dominated the pop music scene for years.

Everything she sings turns platinum... Few recording careers in recent history have been as carefully orchestrated. Or, some would say, as blessed with good luck. The truth according to Dion's top management, is a little of both...

— Jon Burlingame, *Variety*, 14 December 1998

(CP Photo/Paul Chiasson)

(Courtesy Bob Massey)

▲ Canadian singer/songwriter **Alanis Morissette** won three Grammy awards and sold over 16 million copies of her album, *Jagged Little Pill*.

"Most people's growth is done in private; an artist's growth is done in public. I thank Canada for accepting that in me."

— Alanis Morissette, 1996 Juno Awards

▼ The return of **swing** music and the Big Band sound. The band, *Tyler Yarema and His Rhythm* had the crowd hopping at the Reservoir Lounge in downtown Toronto.

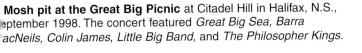

Mosh pit at the Great Big Picnic at Citadel Hill in Halifax, N.S., September 1998. The concert featured *Great Big Sea, Barra MacNeils, Colin James, Little Big Band,* and *The Philosopher Kings*.

Generation X

The media found elements of Coupland's characters' lives in America's youth and labeled them Generation X. This stereo-typical definition leads society to believe that Generation X is made up of cynical, hopeless, frustrated and unmotivated slackers who wear grunge clothing, listen to alternative music and still live at home because they cannot get real jobs. It is a label that has stuck, stereotypes and all.

— *Nevada Outpost*, 1997

(CP Photo/Rene Johnston)

1990
—
1999

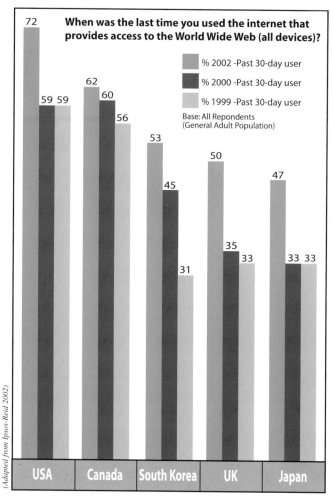

When was the last time you used the internet that provides access to the World Wide Web (all devices)?

- % 2002 -Past 30-day user
- % 2000 -Past 30-day user
- % 1999 -Past 30-day user

Base: All Repondents (General Adult Population)

(Adapted from Ipsos-Reid 2002)

	USA	Canada	South Korea	UK	Japan
2002	72	62	53	50	47
2000	59	60	45	35	33
1999	59	56	31	33	33

▲ **Computers** are now an integral part of most schools.

Internet Game Addiction Concerns:

- Declining grades
- Less investment in relationships with boyfriend or girlfriend
- Withdrawal from all campus social activities and events
- General apathy, edginess, or irritability when off-line (cybershakes)
- Denial of seriousness of the problem
- Rationalizing what they learn on the Net is superior to their classes
- Lying about how much time they spend online and what they do there...

— Dr. Kimberly Young, executive director, Centre for Online Addiction, 2003

...It seems likely that 2000 will be remembered as the year when governments started to regulate cyberspace in earnest; and forgot...that the reason the worldwide network became such an innovative force at all was a healthy mix of self regulation and no regulation....

— "Stop Signs on the Web," *The Economist,* 11 January 2001

Online Job Hunting Now Among Most Popular Online Activities

One-half of Canadian adults with Internet access have looked at online job postings.

— *Ipsos Reid,* 24 July 200(

Love at First Byte

A new sociology, a huge business: How on-line personals have changed the dating game... Singles worldwide are flocking to on-line dating sites, paying $30 or more a month for the services...what's most fascinating is the cultural shift. On-line personals have, remarkably, shaken off the sleazy reputation of newspaper classifieds...This is also a generational shift...

"There are a number of trends," says Tim Sullivan, president of the Dallas based Match.com. "People are getting married later, moving around for work more often, and not marrying in college as frequently. Plus, many young people are sitting at a screen all day long, so it's convenience — they don't have as much time to look, yet there are more singles than ever to sift through..."

— *Report on Business,* October 2002

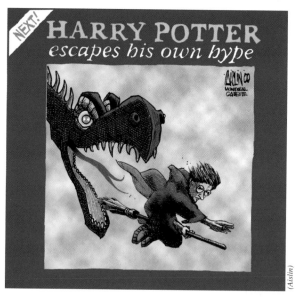

▲ J. K. Rowling's books about child wizard **Harry Potter** proved that children would turn off the TV to read "a chapter book" of over 500 page Worldwide sales of the first four books topped 190 million copies.

renewed interest in **healthy living** and the search for inner
[pea]ce encouraged many people to explore disciplines such as
[yog]a or pilates. Fast food chains changed their menus to include
[sala]ds and other healthy foods.

▲ **"Hangin' out at the mall"** is as popular as ever.

"**My Big Fat Greek Wedding** uses stereotypes in a delightful blend of sweet
[ro]mance and lovingly dished out humour," wrote Joshua Tyler of *Film Hobbit*.
[Wi]nnipeg writer/actor Nia Vardalos became an overnight sensation when her play
[wa]s turned into the hit romantic comedy of 2002, winning the People's Choice
[A]ward for that year. She followed her movie success with the TV sitcom *My Big
[Fa]t Greek Life*. Other Canadian movie successes of 2002 included: *Men with
[Br]ooms*, starring Leslie Neilsen and Paul Gross; and the *Red Green* movie.

When an outbreak of Severe Acute Respiratory
Syndrome (SARS) in Toronto in March 2003 hurt the
local economy, **Mike Myers** of *Wayne's World* and
Austin Powers fame downplayed SARS on U.S. TV.

"…Toronto is safe. I'm not much of a politician and
I'm not super great at doing stuff like this but I just
wanted to say Toronto's gotten a bit of a bad rap
from the media and it's kinda unfair," Myers said…

— "Actor Mike Myers says 'Toronto is safe,'" *Ottawa
Citizen,* 13 May 2003

Fans Go Crazy For Avril's Shirt

…About a minute after pop star Avril Lavigne stopped
[s]inging on *Saturday Night Live* in New York City…the
[p]hone started ringing at the Home Hardware store in
[h]er hometown of Napanee…. Callers from just about
everywhere want to know how they can buy a little red
T-shirt just like the one Lavigne wore on the show while
singing two hits.

The little red shirt that had the words "Home
Hardware" in big letters and "Napanee" in little letters
underneath…. People across the country have been
walking into Home Hardware stores and asking about
purchasing one…. It's the kind of publicity money can't
buy…. To buy that kind of advertising time on *Saturday
Night Live* would have cost $1,125,000 U.S….

— *Toronto Star,* 17 January 2003

Canadian Content Still Needs Enforcing Says CFTPA

"Jack Valenti, the president of the Motion Picture Association of America,
told us at our annual conference in Ottawa this past February that no
government can 'order citizens to watch what they do not wish to watch.'
That is true. But what Mr. Valenti neglected to acknowledge is you can
only decide what to watch from the choices you are offered. If you take
away the Canadian content regulation of the Broadcasting Act, you will
not have many Canadian choices."

— Julia Keatley, chair of the CFTPA and
executive producer, Keatley Films Ltd.

Music! Movies! TV Shows!

*Millions of people download them
every day. Is Digital piracy killing
the entertainment industry?*

— *Time,* 5 May 2003

(CP Photo/Richard Lam)

▲ **Historic Hockey Golds at Salt Lake Winter Olympics** In February 2002, fans such as these Vancouverites spilled onto the streets to celebrate the double gold victory of the Canadian Women's and Men's Hockey teams against the U.S. teams. Strangers hugged, sang, and played road hockey at the intersections of Canada's busiest streets. Was it the lucky loonie at centre ice planted by a member of the ice maintenance crew that did the trick?

▲ **Jamie Sale and David Pelletier** There was outrage across the world when Sale and Pelletier lost the gold medal to the Russian team at the XIX Olympic Winter Games in Salt Lake City, Utah. The controversy heated up when the French judge admitted that she had been pressured to vote for the Russians. Almost a week later Jamie and David were awarded a second gold medal in pairs figure skating.

What was the most priceless moment in Canadian sport?

33% Olympic golds in hockey at Salt Lake
29% Henderson's goal in 1972
19% Sale and Pelletier's gold medal performance at Salt Lake
14% Toronto Blue Jays Winning the World Series

— Environics Poll (following the Olympics) 2002

SKATEGATE!

OUTRAGE ON THE HOME FRONT

— *Ottawa Sun*, 13 February 2002

"…if medals were awarded for good sportsmanship, the Canadian national anthem would be playing while Sale and Pelletier stood atop the podium."

— *Moose Jaw Times Herald*, February 2002

WEIR SO GREAT!

— *Toronto Star*, 14 April 2003

(CP Photo/Frank Gunn)

▸ **Mike Weir**, the first Canadian to win the Master's Golf Tournament wears the coveted green jacket.

Move over Paul Henderson: ... Canada has a new hockey hero

— Mark MacKinnon, *Globe and Mail*, 12 May 2003

CANADA'S FIRST MAN TO TAKE A MAJOR

…Was it the greatest or most prestigious sporting accomplishment ever by a Canadian in an individual sport? Very likely, for in a worldwide game there is no title more coveted than the one Weir won yesterday with a performance that will forever be part of the sport's lore.

— Cam Cole, *National Post*, 14 April 2003

The son of immigrant parents from Barbados, he wobbled onto the ice for the first time as an eight year old in a Scarborough rink. Twenty years later, the NHL star scores a heart-stopping overtime goal to win gold for Canada at the world championships.…"We used to call him the Zamboni," Mrs. Carter said of her son's tendency to slide across the ice "on his buttocks…" [added his father]

— "A hockey hero's wobbly start," Jeff Gray, *Globe and Mail*, 13 M. 2003

What Candians rely on for accurate news and information

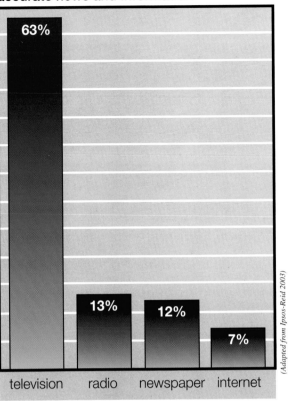

(Adapted from Ipsos-Reid 2003)

- television: 63%
- radio: 13%
- newspaper: 12%
- internet: 7%

Increasing social awareness Kasey Holberton, left, ∎d Jeff Webster, address high school students at a ∎RTY (Prevent Alcohol and Risk Related Trauma in ∎uth) meeting in Calgary, April 2003. Both became ∎ndicapped as a result of alcohol/drug related accidents.

Reporting on the Iraq War

The lines between news and entertainment have been obliterated...

— A. Zerbisias, *Toronto Star,* 25 March 2003

...In Doha, held on a slick $200,000 set designed by a Hollywood consultant, each briefing so far has begun with a bullish statement about the state of war and videos depicting precision bombing by the U.S.-led forces.

— *Reuters,* 30 March 2003

...There are two kinds of forward reporters: the official embeds with units on the ground in Iraq who know only the details of the action they see, and those posted to military press centres...who only know what they are told... This is the job: not to cover war but to cover the news conference about the war. This is likely the Schwarzkopf effect. During Gulf I, he made the daily briefing good television — you had a star.... In some weird way, in our weird war in the weird media bunker, the briefers become a kind of stand-in for the troops themselves... Possibly everyone is media trained.

— Michael Wolff, *New York,* 6 April 2003

...CBC Newsworld...chose to air disturbing video images originating with Iraqi state television, depicting the bloodied corpses of roughly five U.S. troops killed in a battle... Meanwhile CNN and other U.S. outlets abided by the request, airing only a very few, heavily doctored pictures of the dead.

"[A]mong North American magazines and newspapers a tradition dates at least as far back as World War II of modifying or censoring the pictures of war and its more harrowing consequences. No war could sustain public support if all the most gruesome images were broadcast without pause."... [Roy Peter Clark, vice-president of the Poynter Institute]

— *Toronto Star,* 25 March 2003

You say paternal...and I say relax

Although the ever-growing influence of American capitalism and popular culture cannot be denied, there are still many differences between the social values of Americans and Canadians....

In general, Americans continue to adhere to the values of modernity, putting their emphasis on achievement and ostentatious consumption; they embrace patriarchy, hierarchy, and traditional moral or religious beliefs and practice.... Our emphasis is shifting toward greater well-being, harmony and a less traditional quest for spiritual meaning....

The greater Canadian acceptance of diversity, as well as our aversion to ardent patriotism, does not, however, diminish our feelings as a nation....

While the recent popularity of...[the] I-am-Canadian character may suggest that Canadians take greater pride in their country, "Joe" is more a parody than an example of a patriot....

— Michael Adams and Amy Langstaff of Environics Research Group, *Globe and Mail,* 26 July 2000

Index